SHIPS IN THE DESERT

JEFF FEARNSIDE

sfwp.com

Advance Praise

"Informative, impassioned, and urgent… *Ships in the Desert* is a clarion call to protect and treasure the 'grain of gold' in 'every drop of water,' to honor our collective humanity, and to acknowledge the grievous losses and courageous hopes that bind us."
—Kim Barnes, Pulitzer Prize Finalist, author of *In the Wilderness: Coming of Age in Unknown Country*

"An intimate and effortlessly wide-ranging account of one of the gravest—and saddest—anthropogenic disasters in the world. Jeff Fearnside is a writer of genuine decency, and this is a very admirable book."
—Tom Bissell, author of *Chasing the Sea* and *Apostle*

"Continu[ing] the tradition of great writers such as Montaigne, Wendell Berry, and Annie Dillard, Jeff Fearnside takes us on a journey in a place many of us think of as 'over there.' By the end, readers will come to see that over there is never really far away."
—Taylor Brorby, author of *Boys and Oil*

"Fearnside explores environmental degradation and religious tensions, the powerful influence of a Soviet past on the present, and what it means to be a teacher in a foreign land. There is much in this book to be admired."
—Kurt Caswell, winner of the 2008 River Teeth Nonfiction Book Prize, and author of *Laika's Window: The Legacy of a Soviet Space Dog*

"In rich, searching essays… [Fearnside] shows us that we have much to learn from the realities of a country most Americans can't find on a map, revealing how we are connected, and all responsible for living with integrity."
—Michael Copperman, author of *Teacher: Two Years in the Mississippi Delta*

"In this thoughtful essay collection drawn from his Peace Corps career, Jeff Fearnside presents colorful glimpses and measured observations of life, politics, religion, and teaching in one of the lesser-known 'stans' of Central Asia."
—John Daniel, author of *Oregon Rivers* and *The Far Corner: Northwestern Views on Land, Life, and Literature*

"In *Ships in the Desert*, Jeff Fearnside explores Central Asia with great sensitivity.... Timely, illuminating, and wise, it intimately braids the personal with the political into a compelling study of place and our wider engagement with the world."
—Julian Hoffman, author of *Irreplaceable* and *The Small Heart of Things*

"Jeff Fearnside has written a remarkable book of essays, particularly for the central chapter, the title essay, 'Ships in the Desert,'... revealed as a passionate, argumentative, yet thoughtful idealist, a small 'd' democrat. I recommend this wonderful book without hesitation."
—John Keeble, author of *Yellowfish* and *The Appointment: The Tale of Adaline Carson*

"If you've ever lived and worked in a country other than your own and come to love some of the traditions and people of that place with all your heart, this book will speak to you."
—Carolyn Kremers, former Fulbright Scholar in Russia, author of *Place of the Pretend People* and *Upriver*

"Fearnside illuminates the forces behind the demise Central Asia's Aral Sea and questions what we should be learning from, and teaching to, a region struggling to balance the outflow of water with the inflow of western missionaries and oilmen."
—Ruby McConnell, author of *Ground Truth: A Geological Survey of a Life*

"Think is what Jeff Fearnside does spectacularly well. With rare compassion and intelligence, he delves into the complexities of Kazakhstan, revealing a fascinating view of a country now tragically in the news."
—Kathleen Dean Moore, author of *Great Tide Rising*

"*Ships in the Desert* offers a nuanced picture of Kazakhstan and Central Asia through stunning vignettes and powerful research about Kazakhstanis, their politics, and, at times, their poisoned landscapes…, helping us empathize and care about a nation so far away."
—Sean Prentiss, award-winning author of *Finding Abbey: The Search for Edward Abbey and His Hidden Desert Grave* and returned Peace Corps volunteer

"Part memoir, part travelogue, part manifesto, Jeff Fearnside's *Ships in the Desert* unfolds in a series of vivid vignettes that bring the culture and history of Central Asia to life…. I learned a lot from this engaging and valuable book."
—Scott Slovic, University Distinguished Professor of Environmental Humanities, University of Idaho

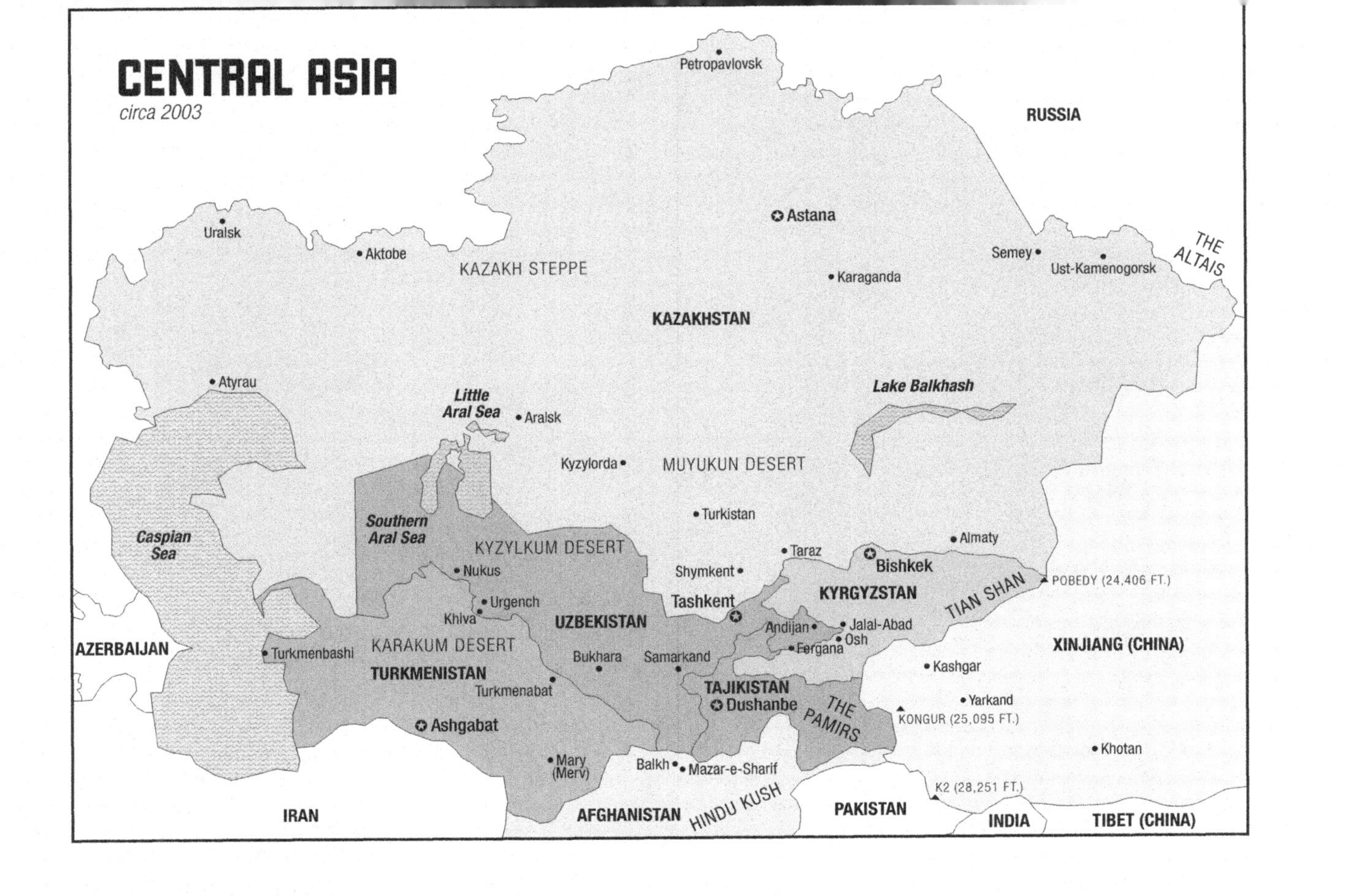
CENTRAL ASIA
circa 2003
RUSSIA
Petropavlovsk
Astana
Uralsk
Aktobe
KAZAKH STEPPE
Semey
Ust-Kamenogorsk
THE ALTAIS
Karaganda
KAZAKHSTAN
Atyrau
Little Aral Sea
Aralsk
Lake Balkhash
Kyzylorda
MUYUKUN DESERT
Turkistan
Caspian Sea
Southern Aral Sea
KYZYLKUM DESERT
Almaty
Taraz
Bishkek
Shymkent
Nukus
KYRGYZSTAN
POBEDY (24,406 FT.)
TIAN SHAN
Tashkent
Urgench
Khiva
UZBEKISTAN
Andijan
Jalal-Abad
Osh
Fergana
AZERBAIJAN
Turkmenbashi
KARAKUM DESERT
XINJIANG (CHINA)
Bukhara
Samarkand
Kashgar
TURKMENISTAN
Turkmenabat
TAJIKISTAN
Dushanbe
THE PAMIRS
Yarkand
KONGUR (25,095 FT.)
Ashgabat
Khotan
Mary (Merv)
Balkh
Mazar-e-Sharif
K2 (28,251 FT.)
IRAN
AFGHANISTAN
HINDU KUSH
PAKISTAN
INDIA
TIBET (CHINA)

Library of Congress Cataloging-in-Publication Data

Names: Fearnside, Jeff, author.
Title: Ships in the desert / Jeff Fearnside.
Description: Santa Fe, NM : SFWP, [2022] | Includes bibliographical references. | Summary: "In this linked essay collection, award-winning author Jeff Fearnside analyzes his four years as an educator on the Great Silk Road, primarily in Kazakhstan. Peeling back the layers of culture, environment, and history that define the country and its people, Fearnside creates a compelling narrative about this faraway land and soon realizes how the local, personal stories are, in fact, global stories. Fearnside sees firsthand the unnatural disaster of the Aral Sea-a man-made environmental crisis that has devastated the region and impacts the entire world. He examines the sometimes controversial ethics of Western missionaries, and reflects on personal and social change once he returns to the States. Ships in the Desert explores universal issues of religious bigotry, cultural intolerance, environmental degradation, and how a battle over water rights led to a catastrophe that is now being repeated around the world"—Provided by publisher.
Identifiers: LCCN 2021043648 (print) | LCCN 2021043649 (ebook) | ISBN 9781951631154 (trade paperback) | ISBN 9781951631161 (ebook)
Subjects: LCSH: Fearnside, Jeff—Travel—Asia, Central. | Americans—Asia, Central. | Asia, Central—Description and travel. | Silk Road—Description and travel. | BISAC: TRAVEL / Essays & Travelogues | TRAVEL / Asia / Central
Classification: LCC DS327.8 .F43 2022 (print) | LCC DS327.8 (ebook) | DDC 915.80408913—dc23/eng/20220520
LC record available at https://lccn.loc.gov/2021043648
LC ebook record available at https://lccn.loc.gov/2021043649

Published by SFWP
369 Montezuma Ave. #350
Santa Fe, NM 87501
(505) 428-9045
www.sfwp.com

Contents

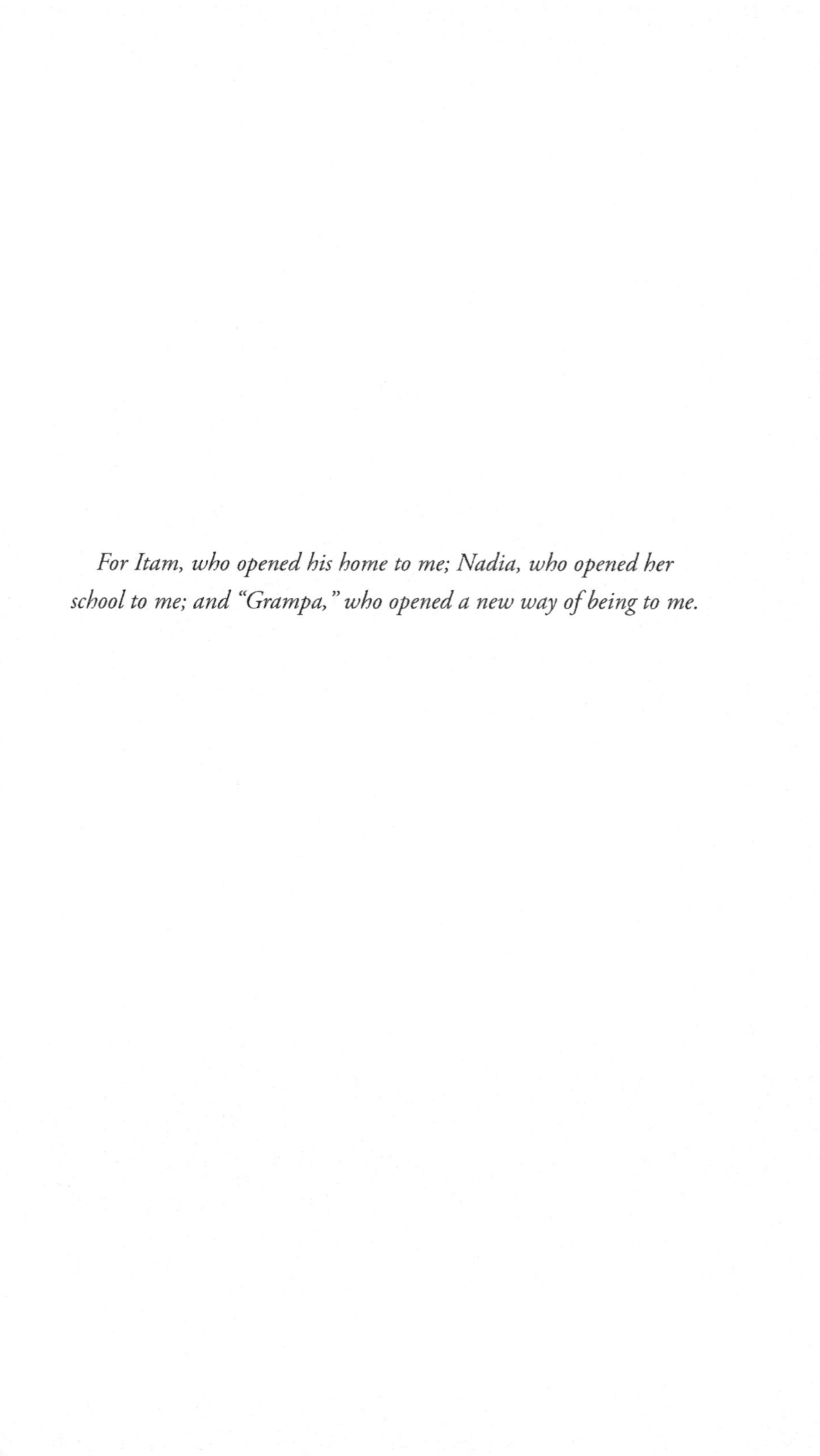

For Itam, who opened his home to me; Nadia, who opened her school to me; and "Grampa," who opened a new way of being to me.

Nothing is farther away than yesterday;
nothing is closer than tomorrow.

—Kazakh proverb

PREFACE

I served as a U.S. Peace Corps volunteer teaching English in Kazakhstan from 2002 to 2004. My motivations for doing so were many. I had long held an interest in other cultures, and the lure of not just travelling through but living in a foreign country was strong. And I was (and remain) an unabashed idealist. I believe in the Peace Corps' first two goals: to help the peoples of interested countries in meeting their need for trained men and women, and to help promote a better understanding of Americans on the part of the peoples served. Though I sometimes struggled to adapt to my new environment, I took my role as a cultural ambassador seriously.

The Peace Corps has a third goal: to help promote a better understanding of other peoples on the part of Americans. To a large degree, this has led me to write about my experiences in Kazakhstan. Even in this age of the internet, Americans know surprisingly little of substance about my host country.

I ended up living there for almost four years, working in Kyrgyzstan as well, and travelling along the Silk Road throughout Muslim Asia, in Turkey, Uzbekistan, Northern India, and the Xinjiang Province of China. That part of the world I experienced and the people I met there were nothing like too many media outlets in the U.S.—whether in ignorance, for the sake of ratings, or willfully, for political reasons—have presented them to be. What I found, and what I hope this book provides, is a more nuanced picture of Muslims in general.

Extremists do exist, who for their own inscrutable reasons are bent on sowing animosity, discord, and even terror, and I am resolutely against such extremism in any form. There is a reason for their name—they represent the extreme beliefs and actions of any group of people. They are not representative of the majority. Central Asia, where I spent most of my time overseas, has long been known for its hospitality. Central Asians' views of religion tend to be pragmatic rather than ideological. Sufi missionaries introduced Islam to the region more than a millennium ago, and the moderating influence of Sufism has been felt there ever since.

That's not to say life is perfect in that part of the world, for it certainly is not. Yet one thing seems clear to me: the issues there are representative of those we face everywhere, including the United States—social justice issues, such as religious bigotry and cultural intolerance, and environmental issues, such as industrial-technological attitudes that treat the world solely as an inexhaustible material storehouse and questions of water rights in a time where access to clean, adequate amounts of that life-sustaining liquid is increasingly becoming problematic for millions of people.

An encyclopedia of many volumes could be written about all this. May this book offer some beginning points in much broader conversations, the first stirrings to change our attitudes, if necessary, and to take action.

It should be noted that geographically, Central Asia has been variously defined. When speaking of it historically, I'm referring to the region known well into the twentieth century as Turkestan ("The Land of the Turks"), which was composed of all or part of today's Afghanistan, Kazakhstan, Kyrgyzstan, Tajikistan, Turkmenistan, Uzbekistan, and China's autonomous Xinjiang province, or Chinese Turkestan. When speaking of current developments, however, I'm referring specifically to the middle five of those countries, or the five post-Soviet "'stans."

Central Asians are, despite their nationalistic pride, far more similar than their different ethnic names would suggest. For example, the Kazakhs and Uzbeks were the same people until what was essentially a family feud split them in 1468, and the Kazakh, Kyrgyz, Turkmen, and Uzbek languages are all Turkic tongues. None of today's five post-Soviet Central Asian countries existed as separate political entities named after any form of their respective ethnic groups until the 1920s; before then, they were historically part of Turkestan. Today's somewhat arbitrary borders in Central Asia are the legacy of Stalin's ploys to divide and conquer the region's people.

Regarding personal names, I have, where it seemed necessary, changed those of certain people portrayed here in order to protect their identities. In every other way, details are as accurate as I remember them, and as I had recorded them at the time they occurred.

I wish to thank the journals in which the chapters of this book originally appeared, sometimes in slightly different forms:

"Itam" first appeared in *A Life Inspired: Tales of Peace Corps Service* (U.S. Peace Corps); "Ships in the Desert" first appeared in *New Madrid*; "The Missionary Position: A Personal Exploration of the Politics of Persuasion in Central Asia" first appeared in *Rock & Sling: A Journal of Literature, Art, and Faith*; "More than Tenge and Tiyn" first appeared in *Silk Road Review*; "Place as Self" first appeared in *ISLE: Interdisciplinary Studies in Literature and Environment*; "View from a Bridge" first appeared in *Etude: New Voices in Literary Nonfiction*; and "Postoyanstvo pamyati (The Persistence of Memory)" first appeared in *Postcard Poems and Prose Magazine.*

I also thank the Bernheim Arboretum and Research Forest in Clermont, Kentucky, and the Mary Anderson Center for the Arts in Mount St. Francis, Indiana, for awarding writing fellowships that allowed time and support to complete a portion of this manuscript;

editor Tara Masih, for selecting "Itam" an Honorable Mention for the Tara L. Masih Intercultural Essay Prize and subsequently reprinting it in *The Chalk Circle: Intercultural Prizewinning Essays* (Wyatt-MacKenzie Publishing); and the editors of *New Madrid*, for nominating "Ships in the Desert" for a Pushcart Prize.

Most importantly, I thank my many friends and colleagues of various nationalities from my time overseas, too numerous to list individually here, though I would be remiss if I didn't specifically mention my parents; my host family during Peace Corps training in Kazakhstan, the Turganovs; my teaching counterpart Nadia Amanbaeva; fellow volunteers and critical readers par excellence Joshua Lamb and Dr. Richard "Grampa" Spear; my astute and inspiring publisher Andrew Gifford and copyeditor Brenna Ebner; and my greatest helper and supporter in all areas of my life: my wife Valentina. Passages from the book *Aralskaya Katastrofa* (*The Aral Catastrophe*) as well as all other phrases in Russian were translated by Valentina and myself.

Jeff Fearnside, July 2022

ITAM

I met him when he came to pick me up from the Soviet-era sanatorium, a health spa where I had spent my first three days in Kazakhstan learning as quickly as possible some of the complexities of this vast country. I hadn't known a word in Russian before I arrived, and I struggled to pronounce properly my simple greeting to him and his wife, Farida.

"Zdravstvuite, menya zovut Jeff." (Hello, my name is Jeff.)

They both smiled politely and introduced themselves but said nothing more.

It was early June but already hot. The ride to my new home, a village on the edge of the foothills to the snow-peaked Tian Shan ("Celestial Mountains"), took two hours. Along the way, Farida stopped to do some shopping. While we waited, Itam played a battered tape of Uyghur music, which I liked: the exotic melodies and driving, percussive rhythms wrapped in a contemporary pop sound.

Here, we first used the goulash of languages that would see us through the next two and a half months of my training—a mix of Russian, English, German, and gesture. Itam had studied German at university many years before, and I had taken a semester of it nearly as long ago. He had picked up some English from his two sons who were studying it, while I took Russian lessons every day.

He always spoke slowly and clearly to me in Russian, which I appreciated. But, like many people, he also had the peculiar habit of speaking extremely loudly, as if sheer volume would somehow help me understand better.

"Jeffrey, come!" he boomed at mealtimes, his light green eyes laughing. "Kushai, kushai!" It would become a familiar refrain—eat, eat!—along with chai pei (drink tea) and chut-chut. Literally, chut-chut means "a little," but in Kazakhstan there's no such thing as a little when it comes to food or drink. Though Kazakhstan is a Muslim country, much of the population drinks, perhaps a hangover from Soviet times. While Itam occasionally enjoyed vodka, he did so moderately, and he never pressured me to join him.

I called him my host father, but he was only eight years older than I, so he was really more like a protective older brother. He taught me the finer points about local customs: gently chiding me for shaking water from my hands after I washed them (Uyghurs believe this brings misfortune) and showing me how to give handshakes the Central Asian way—lightly but warmly, with free hands holding each other's forearms to show respect. When I discovered that I had forgotten to bring a handkerchief with me, he gave me one of his. In every way, he made a special effort to include me in his life and the life of his family.

"Jeffrey!" he boomed. "You, me, go arbeiten." He always used the German word for "to work," though I understood the Russian—rabotat—just as well. He was a veterinarian, and I once watched as he peered into cows' eyes, administered shots, and rubbed ointment into their sores.

On another occasion, he and Farida had me dress in my best for a Uyghur wedding.

Ethnic Uyghurs trace their roots to the primarily Muslim Xinjiang province of China and are closely related to the Turkic peoples of Central Asia. This wedding featured some folk music similar to what I had heard on my first ride with Itam. They also played Russian rock and roll and, more than once, the extended live version of the Eagles' "Hotel California."

At first, I felt shy and resisted invitations to join in the dancing. I sat on the periphery and watched, enjoying the seemingly bottomless portions of heavily mayonnaised salads and appetizers that were a full meal to me, though they were really just the warm-up to the actual meal. Eventually I was moved to join the happy throng, the men in suits, the women in glittering dresses, their arms gracefully twining and untwining above their heads. We danced all through the evening and into the next morning.

※

The days moved slowly that summer in my village. It wasn't exactly a place that time had passed by, but certainly only fingers of modernity had managed to slip in under the blanket of time. My family had electricity and a television, but, like most of their fellow villagers, no telephone. Water had to be carried from a well half a kilometer away; hot water was made by boiling it or, for outdoor showers, by leaving a barrel exposed to the sun all day.

The family's fortune, if counted in hard currency, was a trifle. Itam's income barely met their needs. But as with Central Asian peoples since before recorded history, their real wealth was measured in the richness of their family life and in animals—in their case, sheep.

Toward the end of my stay, they needed to sell five sheep from their flock to pay for the education of their children—two sons, Malik and Adik, and a daughter, Takmina—for the coming year. I was invited along to help catch the animals. We hopped onto a small horse-drawn cart and slowly clopped up the road to the pasture where two pastukhi, or shepherds, were overseeing the common herd. Itam's father-in-law, who knew the exact age, sex, and condition of each of their animals by sight, chose the best from among them. Itam and his sons and I chased them down, tied them up, and placed them in the cart.

Clouds of dust rose into the sky, the sun fell toward the horizon, and the nearby mountains faded into a hazy blue and then an indistinct shadow. It was dark when we rode back down the road toward home. I felt bad for the poor sheep lying next to me, but I felt good knowing that we were taking part in a cycle of life that had been played out for centuries here—knowing that Malik and Adik would be able to continue studying English, that Takmina would gain a marketable skill in learning to cut and style hair before eventually going on to university as well.

I also sensed that Itam was proud of me for helping his family in this way. My feeling about this only increased on his forty-fifth birthday, the first and only time I ever saw him drunk.

He came in late for dinner, having been out celebrating with two friends from his university days. While Farida ladled out soup and prepared a pot of strong black tea, Itam rambled on, more emotional than usual. His family, unaccustomed to this, largely remained quiet. Finally, he put down his spoon and looked directly at me, struggling for words.

"Moe serdtse …" he said at last, pressing his hand to his chest. When I said I didn't understand, he repeated it in English. "My … my heart …"

I was touched. He seemed to be trying to tell me how much he would miss me. I placed my hand on his forearm and squeezed.

※

My training was over, and the time to leave for my assignment as a full-fledged volunteer had arrived. All the family came to see me off, all except for Itam. He had planned his vacation for this time and was away again with his university friends.

I tried to give back Itam's handkerchief, but Farida refused, saying that I would need it. She also promised that Itam would meet me at the train station.

To my disappointment, he never showed up. But I left with hugs from the rest of the family and more memories than it seemed two and a half months could possibly provide.

After a fifteen-hour train ride, I arrived at my new home, Shymkent. Far from being the dangerous place I had been warned of ("Texas" my family called it, for they believed it was like the Wild West), I found this sprawling, low-rise city colorful and friendly. Its tree-lined streets were cool and dotted with many interesting cafés. The university where I would teach was small, but its students were enthusiastic. I looked forward to a bright two years of work.

This exciting time was darkened by some terrible news: Itam had died the day after I left. Previously unknown to everyone, he'd had a heart condition, which became lethal when combined with his recent celebrations.

I remembered him talking of his heart and was shocked to realize he had been trying to tell us of feeling pains in his chest. In hindsight, it seems we might have caught this, but at the time it was the furthest notion from our minds. He was middle-aged and seemingly in perfect health. Only days before I had wrestled sheep to the ground with him.

I learned another hard lesson in hindsight when I found that I didn't have a single photograph of Itam. I had photos of the rest of the family, my Peace Corps friends, some village children, my pupils, even a few random pastukhi. I must have assumed that Itam would always be around, that I would have plenty of chances to catch him in just the right moment.

The only tangible remembrance I had was his handkerchief.

It's funny how small, seemingly insignificant moments in our lives can take on such meaning later. If I had brought a handkerchief with me to Kazakhstan, then I would have nothing to remember Itam by.

There's nothing obviously extraordinary about it. It's just a simple piece of cloth, probably bought at the local bazaar for a few tenge coins. Yet when I look at it, I see pictures woven into the cotton: I see laughing, light green eyes and in them the reflection of lush green foothills, snow-peaked mountains, dusty pastures, hazy steppe sunsets. And darkness. But in that darkness rings the clip-clop of horse's hooves, the trill of Uyghur wedding music, a voice booming "Jeffrey!" and I feel that at any moment, I might stand up and dance.

SHIPS IN THE DESERT

Two images remain with me:

The first is of the Technicolor tile mosaic covering the entire back wall of the waiting room in Aralsk's century-old railway station. Strong men and women, faithfully portrayed in the Soviet realist style, haul in nets teeming with fish and load them onto waiting railway cars. Large Cyrillic script spells out the reason for their industry: "In response to Lenin's letter, let's load fourteen train wagons of fish." The mural is a tribute to the time when Aralsk's citizens helped feed a starving young Soviet nation during a famine. It's a tribute to the life-giving bounty of the Aral Sea.

The second is of a fleet of rusting Soviet fishing ships, hammer and sickle still clearly discernible on many, sitting bolt upright in desert sands as if plowing through ocean waves. At that time, I had already lived for almost a year and would live for another three in beautiful, crazy, haunting, surreal Kazakhstan. But the sight of those ships, so lost no storm could have put them there, so dead yet so apparently alive, was the most beautiful, the most surreal. The story of how they got there is certainly the most crazy, no small boast in a land of storied fighting, infighting, greed, and corruption. That it has haunted me is why I had to write this.

The Aral Sea disaster is one of the worst human-caused environmental catastrophes of the past century, perhaps the worst. In only four decades, what was the world's fourth-largest inland body of water shrank to a mere 10 percent of its former volume. Average salinity sextupled, and its once flourishing fishing industry was destroyed. Agrochemicals exposed on the dry seabed easily found their way into the surrounding environment; the region's people now suffer from some of the highest rates of cancer and infant mortality in the world. Despite the dramatic scope of all this, like something from a science fiction novel, it's surprising how little-known the disaster remains.

Before the September 11 tragedy and our two subsequent wars, few Americans had even heard of Kazakhstan or Uzbekistan, the two countries that share the sea. Now many have, but mainly from seeing them at the edges of maps in newspapers or hearing scraps about them in newscasts, between much larger chunks about Afghanistan and Pakistan. My experience has been that most Americans, even those who are educated and well-traveled, confuse *all* the Central Asian countries with these other two 'stans. Mentioning the Aral Sea doesn't clear the confusion.

Even in Shymkent, Kazakhstan, when I would ask my university students about this disaster taking place in their own country, almost none knew that the sea had become so dried up it had split into two sections (it has since split into three). A couple who did know confidently told of a dike project to save the smaller northern portion, or Little Aral—a project that had already failed twice. Shymkent was then only some eight hundred kilometers from the sea, but based on the knowledge and interest of the local people, one might have thought the Aral was on another planet.

Sadder yet was hearing of the older generation still living in Aralsk, the former bustling fishing port, who, because the waters had retreated so far away, refused to believe the sea still existed. To them, it hadn't disappeared metaphorically; old villagers in Kazakhstan don't think this way. The sea was physically gone forever. And when looking at the rusting hulls of ships mired in the dry harbor, and then beyond them across windswept sand—the former seabed—stretching all the way to the horizon, who could say they were wrong?

Most importantly, what lessons does the Aral Sea disaster have to teach the rest of the world? Frighteningly, many. It's not the unique result of former Soviet megalomania, shortsightedness, or excess. Until only recently, the problem had steadily worsened since the collapse of the Soviet Union, due to the inability of all the countries involved—formerly republics in the same country—to work together. America has its own Aral Sea—several of them, which somehow have failed to generate the attention that might be expected given the serious implications they hold. And widespread lack of potable water may be the most pressing problem for every country on the planet sooner than most currently recognize. If we're not careful, the twenty-first century could well be defined not by terrorism or the growing disparity between rich and poor but by water wars.

Cutting through choppy waves

At the beginning, you drink water; at the end, you drink poison.
—Uzbek proverb

In early May 2003, a small group of colleagues and I living in Kazakhstan decided to visit the sea before it disappeared completely. So from the medieval city of Turkistan, we hopped aboard an overnight train for a modern nightmare.

Getting to the sea was never easy even before it began shrinking. It lies in the heart of the Eurasian landmass—south of Russia, east of the Caspian Sea, and north and west of the towering mountain ranges that separate Central Asia from China and the Indian subcontinent—surrounded by inhospitable deserts and lonely steppes. For some seventy years, it remained behind the Iron Curtain, inaccessible to foreigners. Though both of its major ports, Aralsk in the north and Muynak in the south, were linked by rail to the rest of the Soviet Union, they were far from any other cities of consequence.

Even before arriving in Aralsk, we could see signs of the disaster right outside our train window. All along the railway, salt covered the sandy earth for scores of kilometers. More troubling, I knew it wasn't just salt but also a dry cocktail of chemicals—fertilizers, pesticides, herbicides, and defoliants—that for decades had washed from farms in the watershed.

We were met at Aralsk's train station by Jonathan and Leah, Peace Corps volunteers with a Danish-funded NGO project, "From Kattegat to the Aral Sea." When someone commented on all the salt we'd seen, Jonathan replied that recent rains had washed away much of this crust. Still, so much remained that it appeared like a dusting of snow. It was hard to imagine what it must have looked like only a few weeks before. Probably like glare ice.

We breakfasted at Jonathan and Leah's. The meal was simple: instant coffee, flat rounds of lepyoshka bread, and plov, a Central Asian rice dish. Our hosts explained that it was hard to find much more than this in Aralsk's bazaars and stores. We did, however, find sand in the bread. The crunch was startling. Grinding against one's teeth, the grains feel larger than they actually are. The rasp of them was everywhere in our mouths. Jonathan just shrugged.

"This is usual," he said. "Sand gets into everything here."

Gets into, saturates, obliterates. Many of the town's streets appeared to be avenues of sand. They were empty, a discordant sight in a country where walking is a primary mode of transportation for most people, especially in small towns. Buildings were boarded up; trash lay everywhere. It was a postcard of desolation.

We had arranged to hire a four-wheel-drive vehicle from the NGO office. Our driver was an ethnic Kazakh man named Agytai.

He appeared to be in his mid-forties and stood about five feet, five inches tall, with the ruddy cheeks typical of those who spend their lives outdoors, but while he had been raised in the Soviet Union, his Russian evidently didn't get much of a workout anymore. Our Russian certainly wasn't any better, so we understood each other perfectly. Our vehicle was a late 1990s UAZ Hunter, the Russian version of a Jeep. All six of us had to cram inside, but this wasn't unusual in Kazakhstan, even for a trip such as ours. The sea was eighty kilometers from Aralsk as measured directly. By road, it was one hundred bone-rattling kilometers away.

At first, near town, the road was paved, or at least had been in an indeterminate past, flanked by power lines and train tracks, the same tracks that once had carried fish from the Aral to all parts of the Soviet Union. The former sea lay to our left. It was indistinguishable from the desert to our right. On both sides roamed shaggy two-humped Bactrian camels. In this region of Kazakhstan, they're commonly raised for their milk, wool, leather, and meat, though by tradition the local people don't eat them after Nauryz, the Central Asian New Year, which falls on or near the spring equinox. So those we saw were fattening themselves up on saltbush, wormwood, and camel's thorn, safe until winter.

The partially paved road soon ended, giving way to a narrow two-track. We rode on the old seabed now. But while surrounded by sand, the ride was anything but soft; the underlying clay bottom had become rutted during the recent rains. We bounced so badly that our heads bumped the roof of the UAZ. The sensation was akin to cutting through choppy waves. Repeatedly, Agytai apologized for the conditions.

"This is mud," he said. "It's not my fault." But he was grinning widely. And he never slowed down.

⋇

The Aral has existed intermittently for nearly two million years, but its most familiar form dates back to the last ice age ten thousand years ago. From that time until the twentieth century, the sea's level did vary, and irrigation did occasionally contribute to this. But stability was the norm in recent centuries. According to Aral expert Philip Micklin, the level varied only four to four and a half meters from the mid-eighteenth century to 1960. From the beginning of regular and accurate observations of the sea level in 1910 to 1960, it varied less than one meter.

Figures also vary on the sea's area at that time, but even a conservative estimate of 64,500 square kilometers was enough to make it the world's fourth largest inland body of water, behind only the Caspian Sea, Lake Superior, and Lake Victoria. With an average salinity of 1 percent, less than a third as salty as the ocean, it was a freshwater system supporting a diverse and thriving fishery. The sea's fishing fleet caught from forty thousand to fifty thousand metric tons of fish per year, and the fish processing plants in Aralsk and Muynak were among the Soviet Union's largest. Passenger ferries full of happy Soviet tourists plied the waters between these two ports.

The sea was fed primarily by two rivers, the Amu Darya and Syr Darya, famous since antiquity for their great lengths—2,580 kilometers and 2,220 kilometers, respectively. Some scholars have even identified them as two of the four rivers of Paradise. Indeed, the land between them was a sort of paradise, a wedge of life in a harsh environment that harbored a succession of civilizations over the centuries, from elegant Persian Sogdiana to colorful Arab Silk Road kingdoms, from the empires of Genghis Khan and his heirs to the emirate of Bukhara and khanates of Khiva, Kokand, and Samarkand.

Historically, the region's agriculture centered on small farmers, and the coming of the Soviets initially didn't change this much. Peasants were forced into collective farms, often violently, but at home individual families maintained a way of life as they had for centuries, raising a few cows and sheep, cultivating small fields of rice and wheat, and growing their own gardens of cabbages, tomatoes, melons, and grapes, as well as orchards of apples, apricots, cherries, nuts, and pomegranates. The region's fruit in particular was famed for its large size, rich taste, and juiciness; the hot desert sun and cool waters drawn from the Amu Darya and Syr Darya were perfect for this. Because the irrigation was done on a moderate scale, the amount of water taken was never enough to affect the Aral's level seriously. During years of drought the sea's level dropped a meter or two, but during times of heavy precipitation it rose again. Here and there was grown cotton, a plant that demands great amounts of water. Some of these cotton plantations, dating back to tsarist times, were extremely large. But as a whole, the system was more or less in balance.

Then in the 1950s, the Soviet leaders decided to expand cotton production to an industrial scale. Existing fields of other crops and huge new expanses of desert were ripped up for the "white gold." In many areas, cotton was planted right up to the windowsills of homes, displacing gardens. It pressed against the walls of nurseries and schools. Thus, anything sprayed on the cotton was sprayed on the people, even those who didn't directly work with cotton, though that number was few indeed.

The Soviets had created a new sea, a vast body of cotton, and like any sea it required an inflow of water. The largest and most easily accessible sources of this were the Amu Darya and Syr Darya. Thousands of kilometers of new canals were dug in order to irrigate an area larger than Switzerland. By 1990, it had grown to an area larger than Ireland—or approximately the Aral's original size. The new sea had finally supplanted the old one.

At first, however, there was no noticeable effect on the Aral. Water siphoned from the Amu Darya and Syr Darya was balanced by the amount of drainage water flowing back in combined with a decrease in evaporation and filtration—with less water in the rivers, there was less to lose. But more cotton was planted, more water drawn for irrigation, and new systems built that directed the drainage water to wherever was convenient, often the desert, where it completely evaporated or was lost to the sands. Thus, in about 1960, the sea began to shrink. With the exception of the small northern portion, or Little Aral, it has not stopped shrinking since. The shoreline of the larger southern portion, or Southern Aral, has retreated at least 150 kilometers, while the average water level has dropped twenty-two meters.

The once mighty Amu Darya and Syr Darya are but trickles of their former selves. More properly, the latter is a trickle. The former is nearly dead, exhausted along the way. It now never reaches the sea.

⁜

Listening to music on a car ride in Kazakhstan is always sure to evoke a surprise, especially if it's a long ride. Whether listening to the radio, a tape, or a CD, one is likely to hear a sometimes jarring, sometimes divinely juxtaposed mix of Russian pop, Indian film songs, Turkish dance hits, old Soviet ballads, and the occasional homegrown favorite. American tunes can remain popular in Kazakhstan for years after they've been forgotten in America. The three I heard most often in my time there were Louis Armstrong's "What a Wonderful World," Chris de Burgh's "The Lady in Red," and the live version of the Eagles' "Hotel California."

As we were too far out to pull in a radio station, Agytai played a tape, evidently his favorite tape, maybe even his only tape, for it was the only music we would hear for our entire two-and-a-half-hour ride to the sea. Typical of most compilations there, it contained a mix of hits from around the world, including George Harrison's 1987 smash "Got My Mind Set on You." I enjoyed hearing this song again after so many years. Even the second time. But after the third, fourth, and fifth times, it began sounding like a Weird Al Yankovic parody: "This song's just six words long. This song's just six words long ..."

At a certain point, however, the lyrics began taking on almost prophetic connotations. Repeated like a mystic chant, they seemed to have been penned with the Aral Sea exclusively in mind, with their emphasis on "a whole lotta spending money" and "a whole lot of precious time," all in an attempt "to do it, to do it, to do it right."

As to money, a new project primarily funded by the World Bank would cost $85.8 million. By building a modern dam to keep water from draining into the Southern Aral in addition to rebuilding channels, sluices, and other waterworks along the Syr Darya, the project would thus allow the much smaller Little Aral eventually to stabilize. The philosophy behind this was that it was better to save a fraction of the sea than to lose it all. It was an important step, but it didn't address all the causes of the problem, nor would it alleviate the tragic effects. Hospitals and clinics needed to be built, staffed, and supplied, villages modernized with water treatment facilities, new roads, electricity. The bill for all this would total hundreds of millions of dollars. Kazakhstan is now in a position to begin taking up these responsibilities and has the political will to do so, but Uzbekistan flat out doesn't have the cash or the desire to abandon cotton production.

As to time, the region around the Southern Aral is by everyone's estimate locked into its current blight indefinitely. Even the region around the Little Aral could take decades to return to a measure of its former stability.

And after the expenditure of all this money and time, will the job have been done right?

A scam as large as the Aral disaster

If you don't plant cotton, you will be jailed.
If you don't pick cotton, you will be killed.
—Russian proverbs

These two sayings were born out of the Soviet cotton culture, Grigory

Reznichenko relates in his book *Aralskaya Katastrofa* (*The Aral Catastrophe*). Both involve a play on words in the original Russian. In the first, the root word that is repeated twice, posadit, means both "to plant" and "to imprison." In the second proverb, the repeated root word, ubrat, means both "to harvest" and "to kill."

Gallows humor was perhaps the only thing that gave the region's workers any enjoyment or hope.

During harvesting season, homes, factories, schools, and universities were emptied in order to meet the demand for pickers. Some buildings remained empty for weeks until the last boll was plucked from the last thorny plant. One woman I know, Natasha, remembers bleeding fingers from this forced conscription when she was a student, long days under a hot sun and cold nights in an inadequately supplied makeshift dormitory. The students slept on mats laid out in long rows, pressing against each other for warmth, turning as one body at hourly calls to switch sides from a succession of poor, cramped figures. One season, Natasha developed a bad facial twitch from frozen nerves. She ran away to home, and only a doctor's note saved her from being dragged back to the fields by the authorities. She, like the others, was never even paid the promised salary, being told that it was taken to cover her food and housing.

It was essentially state-sponsored slavery. Reznichenko, the leader of a 1988 scientific expedition to study the effects of the Aral disaster, addresses the perverse politics behind this in direct, devastating language unusual even during perestroika:

> Coercion and fear drive people into the fields. Coercion and fear, but certainly not the salary. For the cotton picker, this is low indeed. And the work is exhausting and monotonous. A person must bend down ten thousand to twelve thousand times to fulfill a daily quota. To collect one hundred kilograms, for which you will be paid five rubles [about eight

> U.S. dollars], you must bend twenty-five thousand times. An infernal, forty-degree [Celsius] heat, poisoned earth and plants, and aridity all destroy people's health, especially that of women and children. But the more cotton there is, the happier and richer the country is!

Reznichenko's ironic tone makes it clear that "the country" actually meant an elite tier of well-connected officials. While the vast majority of people in the region never reaped anything but hard work and poor health from the project, those in charge made fortunes in a scam as large as the Aral disaster itself.

The scam was simple: pad the reports of cotton being produced and pocket the extra rubles. That the farmers couldn't possibly raise the harvests being reported wasn't an issue; the targets of each Five-Year Plan were unrealistic to begin with, which only encouraged more report padding. The system measured the quantity of raw cotton produced, not its quality, allowing for shortfalls to be hidden in a number of ways—understating moisture content, for example. Shortfalls at the ginning stage were covered by bribes. Bribery became rampant as more people, often relatives wanting their share, were brought in and higher-level officials bought off. Only in the early 1980s did satellite imagery of a vast area of empty fields reveal the fraud.

Due to the suicides of several key players and a flawed (perhaps purposefully so) investigation, the full scope of the scam will likely never be known, but Tsuneo Tsukatani has reported in his chapter "The Aral Sea and socio-economic development" from *Central Eurasian water crisis: Caspian, Aral, and Dead Seas* that just between 1978 and the beginning of investigations in 1983, the Soviet state was ripped off for 4 billion rubles, or 6.7 billion U.S. dollars.

The Communist Party leader in Uzbekistan, Sharaf Rashidov, oversaw all this, but to show the extent to which such corruption is considered normal, even admired, in Central Asia, Uzbekistan's former president Islam Karimov "rehabilitated" Rashidov. A statue of him now stands in the capital of Tashkent, where a street is named after him as well. He is considered a national hero. When I lived in Shymkent, Kazakhstan, nearly every day I passed by a ten-foot-tall statue shaped in the symbol of cotton, which, appropriately enough, was built around a water-gulping fountain. With such attitudes, it's no wonder there's little desire, political or popular, to curb the production of cotton.

Cotton is, of course, a useful—one might even say an indispensable—agricultural product whose cultivation dates back millennia. Lightweight, soft, and breathable, yet also strong, durable, and versatile, it's perfectly suited for the many goods we make of it, from archival-quality paper to our everyday clothing. But while it may be grown relatively cheaply in terms of money, it costs much more in terms of resources consumed and the effects of such consumption.

Water is the world's most important resource. Cotton demands a staggering amount—in Uzbekistan, the equivalent of nearly twenty-one thousand liters of water is needed to harvest a single kilogram of cotton, based on figures from Juliette Williams of the Environmental Justice Foundation. According to the World Wildlife Fund, a kilogram of conventionally grown cotton can require up to twenty-nine thousand liters of water to produce.

And it ranks among the world's most heavily sprayed crops. Tsukatani, again in the chapter noted above, writes,

> For years, huge overdoses of chemical fertilizers, pesticides, and defoliants have been poured onto the cotton fields [in the Aral basin]. Among them were DDT, BHC, methyl mercaptophos, octamethyl, butifos, milbex, hexachlorane (BHO), phosphamide (dimethoate), phosalone, lenacil, ronit (Ro-Neet), yalan (molinate), sodium TCA, chlorazone, and aldrin. The chemicals are not only discharged into the rivers through drainage canals, but have also filtered through

> to the groundwater layer when the salinated land is flushed by huge amounts of irrigation water, thus creating capillary channels between surface water and groundwater. The capillary action carries groundwater containing minerals and chemicals to the surface, where they are left to accumulate after the evaporation of the water.

Even after DDT and butifos were banned, they were still widely used. The chemicals were applied in such heavy doses that they hung in the air in sheets, diaphanous like mist but which crept like fog.

※

"Do you smoke?" Agytai asked us several times. A couple members of our group did, but they didn't want to light up in such a tight space or delay our trip by stopping. Agytai would consider this for a while, seeming nervous or agitated. Then in ten or fifteen minutes he would repeat, "Do you smoke?"

After riding for about an hour, one of our group finally asked if we could pull over for a cigarette break.

"Oh, what an excellent suggestion!" Agytai exclaimed. It was the most perfect Russian he spoke all day. He pulled over immediately and was puffing on his own cigarette hardly before the engine had died.

While the smokers indulged themselves in their pleasurable addiction, the rest of us stretched our compacted bones and gazed about the surrounding countryside. The vast plain before us not only looked like a desert, it smelled like one. Baked earth and scorching sun. Despite the recent rains, there wasn't even a whiff of sea. Like tourists, we pulled out our cameras and snapped pictures of camels. They were as obliging as cruise liners, those animals known as "ships of the desert." Who could have guessed that today they would be the only ships moving on the Aral Sea?

Poverty, noxious storms, and death from speeding in unstable sands

When we try to pick out anything by itself, we find it hitched to everything else in the Universe.
—John Muir

The Aral Sea issue is a classic example of the interconnectedness of the earth's living systems, and how altering one seemingly small component can produce a tangle of large, drastic effects.

As the sea disappeared, salt levels rose, from a mild 1 percent to a choking 6 percent on average, nearly twice as salty as the ocean, killing the native fish. In the Southern Aral, where salinity is as high as 10 percent, only brine shrimp can survive. The loss of the fishing industry resulted in poverty and massive displacement and relocation. People in the region were not only employed as fishermen but also as sailors, mechanics, dockworkers, and workers in the fish processing plants and shipyards. Nearly all these jobs are gone. The population of Aralsk fell from eighty thousand to thirty thousand, Muynak from forty thousand to ten thousand.

The sea's moderating effect on the regional climate diminished as well. There was far less moisture evaporating into the air to condense as precipitation and smooth variations in temperature. In the 1950s, the number of rainless days a year was only 30. By 1993, it was 120, and today it's up to 150. Summers are hotter and winters colder.

Irrigation in the Aral basin has become a problem not only because it has drained the Aral's primary sources but also for a number of other reasons. The heavy doses of fertilizers, pesticides, herbicides, and defoliants used in the huge, new expanses of agricultural fields (mainly cotton) eventually find their way into the drainage system that feeds the Aral, accumulating on the sea bottom. As the sea dries up, the chemicals lay exposed to the wind, which lifts them—along with salt, dust, and sand—in biblically proportioned noxious storms. Residues from these storms have been measured as far east as the Baltic Sea and as far west as the Pacific Ocean.

The bulk of noxious dust settles in the region immediately surrounding the Aral, primarily to the south and east. As much chemical-laden salt is now dropped on the region's cropland annually as the amount of fish once pulled from the sea. The salt seeps into the groundwater, which has become too brackish to drink. But people still do. Some have nothing else.

The region's irrigation system, much of it built on the antiquated tsarist-era system already in place, was poorly constructed to begin with, and as it aged, very little of it was repaired. Leakage and evaporation are common from these unlined, open channels. In some areas, up to 60 percent of the water drawn for irrigation is lost before it reaches the fields. In other areas, over-irrigation creates runoff, which erodes the soil, clogging both man-made and natural drainages with silt and further reducing the amount of water they can carry.

Loss of fertile soil is another catastrophe in a region that didn't have much to begin with. What is left has become salinized or, in some areas, simply buried by blowing sands. Where it had been hoped would bloom vast fields of "white gold" instead shimmer vast fields of golden desert.

Or black, red, and white.

A new, toxic desert has been created south and east of the sea. It has been called the Aralkum (Aral Sand) or, due to its characteristic crust of chemical salt, the Akkum (White Sand). It is spreading rapidly and merging with the neighboring Karakum (Black Sand), Kyzylkum (Red Sand), and other natural deserts, leading some to believe the region may one day become a single desert, one of the world's largest.

At the same time that vast areas are drying up, other areas are being flooded. In 2020, an earthen dam burst at the Sardoba Reservoir in Uzbekistan, inundating the Syr Darya river basin, killing several people, and forcing the evacuation of tens of thousands of others in Uzbekistan and Kazakhstan. For a time earlier at the Kazakhstan-Uzbekistan border, an impromptu lake formed because the badly eroded Syr Darya could no longer carry its normal load, and when Kyrgyzstan released water from its upstream dam to generate electricity in winter, it simply spilled into this new lake. Local flooding due to over-irrigation and runoff remains a problem in many other areas. None of this water reaches the sea.

⁂

Intimately connected with the sea are the complex river systems that feed it, in particular the delta systems of the Amu Darya and Syr Darya. Like the sea, they are dying. While this has received less attention than the disappearance of the sea itself, the loss is nearly as great, the consequences as harmful. The deltas provided the spawning grounds for many of the Aral's fish, and they were home to a profusion of other flora and fauna, including wild boars, jackals, and the Bukhara red deer, once called "the khan's flower" for its beautiful ocher coat. Livestock pastured there. People hunted, trapped, and harvested reeds for making paper and constructing homes.

The deltas also support tugai forests, dense communities of phreatophytes—deep-rooted plants that drink from the water table—shrubs, reeds, and other tall grasses. These communities are unique to Central Asia. There are now only 10 percent left, and but a fraction of that is assessed to be in very good condition. Of the 173 animal species that once lived primarily in the deltas, only approximately 20 percent have survived. The Caspian tiger is entirely extinct. The Bukhara red deer went extinct in Kazakhstan's tugai but has since been reintroduced there and elsewhere in the Aral basin. Despite slowly increasing numbers, they remain endangered and literally intoxicated—stumbling in a haze of toxic salts.

The deltas no longer act as natural filters, for the dense plant communities are no longer there to retain the soil—yet another system of important natural and commercial benefit that's become a desert of deflated soils and invasive salt- and drought-resistant species. The future prospects of this ecoregion are dim. Almost no virgin tugai forest exists, and what does exist remains only in remnants. While reserves have been established to protect these remnants, they are small, scattered, and insufficiently managed; the World Wildlife Fund doesn't consider them viable for the long-term success of the tugai forests. Habitat destruction continues due to human activities, mainly logging wood for heating and cooking as well as overgrazing of herd animals, though overirrigation for cotton production and the resulting salinization of the soil are ongoing contributing factors.

The irony of all this is that cotton has never become the fat cash cow that many dreamed of. Corrupt officials and well-connected families have grown rich, no doubt, but the crop itself is losing ground. The cotton monoculture created a situation where diseases were able to adapt and increase. Soil fertility dropped due to nutrient depletion and erosion, while the soils became increasingly salinized.

The result? Falling cotton yields. This isn't new; they've been falling for years. Yet while the region's governments continue to praise the economic benefits of growing cotton—defiantly stating that production will not be curtailed for any reason—their people only continue to slide further into poverty. Everything they once raised on their own—animals for meat and dairy products, fruits, grains, and vegetables—they now must buy. But with cotton production falling, they have less money to purchase these staple items. Despair leads to alcoholism. My colleague Jonathan in Aralsk related that this has become so acute, some fishermen resort to drinking "spirits"—rubbing alcohol—or, when they're especially desperate, Kremlin brand cologne.

All this—the intense poverty, terrible water and air quality, and loss of the fishery and thus an important source of protein—has resulted in widespread malnutrition and epidemics of diseases, including anemia, cholera, dysentery, gastritis, hepatitis, jaundice, tuberculosis, typhoid fever, and various cancers. The people of Uzbekistan's Karakalpakstan region suffer the highest rate of throat cancer in the world. Their infant mortality rate is the highest in the former Soviet Union and more than fifteen times higher than in the United States. Nursing children often refuse to drink their mothers' milk because it is too saline. These circumstances have created genetic damage in the Aral basin's people, producing birth defects and leaving each new generation even more susceptible to cancer.

Perhaps most insidious of all is that biological weapons once hidden on a remote Aral island may now be accessible to anyone with the gumption to get them. Ostrov Vozrozhdeniya eerily translates as "Island of Rebirth" or "Renaissance Island." Indeed, the land there may again bloom—unfortunately not with the local flora, which has been decimated, but instead with weaponized plague bacteria.

From 1936 until being abandoned after the Soviet Union's dissolution in 1991, Renaissance Island saw anthrax, plague, smallpox, and half a dozen other diseases tested on a variety of animals: monkeys, donkeys, horses, rabbits, guinea pigs. Humans were also guinea pigs. In 1971, as the Aral lay dying and its ships inevitably swooned to the bottom, a smallpox outbreak triggered by a secret bioweapons field test killed dozens of people in Aralsk.

Three decades later, Renaissance Island became a peninsula linked to Uzbekistan.

Less than a year before my trip to the Aral, from May to July 2002, an American biochemical engineer with the Pentagon's Threat Reduction Agency led an expedition that reportedly cleaned up the last of the biological mess. But given how much material was deposited there in the deepest secrecy—between one hundred and two hundred tons of anthrax alone—many people aren't convinced that everything was found and destroyed.

It's said that the United States won the arms race with the Soviet Union, yet three decades after the latter's demise, the relics of that race remain a threat.

⋇

During our drive, we intermittently saw monuments along the roadside, simple wooden markers adorned with flowers, bright bits of clothing, and photographs.

"These people died because they were riding motorcycles and turned over," Agytai explained as if commenting on the weather.

Of all the health risks caused by the Aral's disappearance, that has to rank as the most oddly tragic: death from speeding in the unstable sands spread along the old sea bed.

We also passed three massive Muslim cemeteries set on hills that once overlooked the sea. Muslim grave markers in Kazakhstan are formed of adobe. It's the custom to show respect by enclosing these over time in domed mausoleums—the larger and more grandly decorated, the greater the respect shown. From a distance, these walled clusters of buildings looked like ancient caravan cities, only eerily devoid of bustle or any activity save that of slow decay in the sun.

The dearly departed citizens resting therein were among the more fortunate. When the region around the Little Aral was declared an ecological disaster zone, seventeen entire villages were moved, their centuries-old cemeteries abandoned, consumed by the trespassing sands.

We drove through two villages that barely remained, Zhambyl and Tastubek. The former, once situated on a small natural harbor, was now the farther from the sea. Only fifteen families remained in the latter, providing some forty-five men to work the last, small fishing fleet.

If we thought that Aralsk had seemed desolate and empty, then we needed to learn a new vocabulary to describe Zhambyl and Tastubek.

With their dilapidated wooden and adobe houses and streets that were nothing more than the spaces between houses, they resembled temporary nineteenth-century expeditionary outposts more than permanent settlements. Once they were among nearly two dozen fishing villages that had thrived in the Little Aral region alone. I wondered how even these two were able to keep going.

"They put some kind of fish in there," Agytai explained. "They didn't know what kind it was."

"What kind?" I persisted.

"Kambala." Flounder. Here he became excited.

"The sea shrank. They put some fish in there. They didn't know what to do with it, how to catch it, but they finally figured it out."

Fishing isn't as simple as throwing out a net and pulling in whatever swims into it. Different fish live at different depths, eat different foods, and require different strategies to catch. Most are highly sensitive to changes in their environment, particularly temperature and salinity, and die if these changes are too great. That's what happened to all the Aral's twenty-four native species. Others are highly resistant to such changes, which is why flounder was introduced into the Aral. However, this new species puzzled the grizzled fishermen. It didn't behave the way they were used to fish behaving. It didn't even look right—flat, its eyes on one side of its head. No one had ever seen such a creature before. Many were revolted at the thought of eating one.

First, they learned how to catch it, and then they trained themselves to eat it. Alien-eyed or not, it was better than starving.

The Aral-eaters

Everything was happening as in a fairytale: everyone did his or her own business, unaware of the result. Millions, tens of millions, of metric tons of cotton finally tipped the scales, overpowered the Aral, and the sea surrendered.

The Aral Sea died solely because of human activities and the leading role played by the Aral-eaters.
—Grigory Reznichenko

There's a serious lack of accountability in regards to the Aral that shows up in two ways. The first involves poor cooperation among the six countries linked to the Aral basin—Afghanistan, Kazakhstan, Kyrgyzstan, Tajikistan, Turkmenistan, and Uzbekistan. Each of these countries relies on water sources that, if nature were allowed to run its normal course, would ultimately feed the Aral. But negotiations for this natural resource are as winding and treacherous as the mountain waterways that provide it.

The Syr Darya begins in Tajikistan, but one of its headwaters is the Naryn River in Kyrgyzstan, where it's used to generate electricity. In summer, when demand for power is lower, the water remains dammed in a reservoir. In winter, when demand for power peaks, water is released through turbines, but this is when the downriver systems can least accept and hold water, resulting in flooding, which angers Kazakhstan and Uzbekistan. Kyrgyzstan says it's simply doing what it needs to do to survive. Despite agreements to store more water in winter, it continues to disregard its commitments. In both instances, only a small portion of water reaches the Aral Sea.

The Amu Darya is formed by the conjunction of two rivers in Tajikistan, though a sizeable portion of its flow—10 percent or more—comes from Afghanistan. It then winds through Turkmenistan and Uzbekistan. All four of these countries claim their share of its waters or headwaters, and if Afghanistan should stabilize after decades of war, its draw on this resource will only increase.

Turkmenistan has made the most egregious claims, not surprising for a country whose now deceased former president-cum-dictator-for-life Saparmurat Niyazov appointed himself "Turkmenbashi," or "Father of All Turkmens"—a title both political and spiritual. There, grand schemes abound, some goofy, some scary. In the capital of Ashgabat, a gold statue of Niyazov slowly revolves with the course of the sun, always facing it. It's forbidden for men to wear long hair and beards or for anyone to listen to car radios. More recently, using the word "coronavirus" was outlawed, for the state naturally has no such cases. And plans call for greater irrigation of the desert to double current cotton production.

Turkmenistan's Karakum Canal is already one of the longest irrigation channels in the world. Completed in the early 1960s, it's considered the primary factor in the Aral's demise. Similar to other such works in Central Asia, half the water flowing along the leaky canal seeps into the desert, which comprises 80 percent of the country. Yet Turkmenistan not only hopes to cultivate new farms in its "virgin lands," it has also begun building a giant reservoir—named Altyn Asyr, or the Golden Age Lake—in its hinterlands in the Karakum desert to create a more secure water supply. Obviously, much water will soak into the thirsty sands and evaporate into the sweltering skies. Exactly how much? How will it affect Uzbekistan downstream? How will the salts and agrochemicals be removed? At what cost? If they know, Turkmen officials aren't saying. The first stage of the project, involving the construction of eight hundred kilometers of unlined canals, was completed in 2009. As of 2021, the "lake" remains essentially nothing but the desert it originally was.

While five of these six countries fighting for water—all but Afghanistan—were ostensibly comrades together behind the Iron Curtain, they now share an ironclad distrust of one another.

The second way that lack of accountability regarding the Aral shows up involves failure to accept responsibility. The easiest way to do this is simply to tell the truth about why this disaster occurred. But many, particularly those who were trained in the Soviet Union, still refuse to admit, despite conclusive evidence to the contrary, that cotton irrigation is to blame.

In the summer of 2002, shortly after I had arrived in Kazakhstan, I listened to a talk in English by a Soviet-era scientist. He said that in the seventeenth century, the Aral Sea didn't exist—it was nothing more than a swamp. The region's climate goes through fifty- to eighty-year cycles, and rises and declines in sea level are a natural part of these cycles. There was no evidence of livestock becoming sick yet, thus showing how reports of agrochemical pollution were wildly exaggerated. Irrigation had been going on for hundreds of years, and it had never affected the sea before. Why were people now claiming it was?

Another creative explanation for the Aral's demise (which I heard from a number of people in the region) is that an as-yet-undiscovered underground channel runs between the Aral and the Caspian seas, siphoning off water to the latter. Though no evidence has ever surfaced to support this, classroom textbooks presented it as a reasonable cause.

In equally creative "solutions" to the problem, the Soviets, in typically grand thinking, considered bombing mountain glaciers in the Tian Shan and Pamirs to release their frozen waters as well as diverting the course of distant Siberian rivers via canals to replenish the Aral.

The latter was actually *seriously* considered, despite the daunting cost and complexity of the proposal and the grave environmental repercussions it would have caused. The idea of diverting a north-flowing river to the southern breadbasket region was first proposed in the 1830s during Tsarist times. A century later, it was revived during Stalin's Soviet Union, though ditched after initial research and planning—not for environmental reasons but because it was deemed too expensive. It was revived again in the 1960s, and in the 1970s the Soviets even dropped several nuclear bombs to test their safety and efficacy in excavation. In all, the project would have required 250 nuclear explosions and the building of twenty-five dams, flooding millions of acres and displacing tens of thousands of people. With warmer fresh water no longer flowing into the Arctic Ocean, it likely would have either grown colder or, due to the lower freezing point from lower salinity, grown warmer, either way resulting in weather changes not just throughout the region but as far away as North America.

Downsizing the canal system that irrigated the cotton fields was out of the question. Strangely, modernizing these canals so that they wasted less water seemed out of the question, too. Water conservation was never included in the grand scheme to grow more cotton. To the Soviet planners' way of thinking, there was plenty of water flowing unproductively through Siberia and wastefully discharging into the Arctic Ocean. Why not use it? Thankfully, this plan was scrapped in 1986, though the idea resurfaced again in 2004 when Russian scientists considered it at the request of Uzbekistan's former President Karimov, in conjunction with other leaders from the region. It then came up yet *again,* this time during the devastating drought of 2010 in Russia, Ukraine, and Kazakhstan. Given that the idea keeps resurrecting itself like an old Hollywood movie monster—seemingly dead and then fully reanimated for the next sequel—it's unclear if we've heard the last on this matter.

To accept the truth about what happened would certainly encourage more realistic solutions to the problem. Why not do so? The answer provides a fascinating glimpse into the politics of disaster. While it's outwardly fashionable to blame Soviet policies for current woes, many government institutions in Central Asia, including health and education, have remained essentially unchanged since independence. The only differences are semantic.

Thus, there's still a need to support the old Soviet line. For much of this century, two of the Aral basin's countries—Kazakhstan and Uzbekistan—were led by men who had been prominent members of the Communist Party in their respective republics in Soviet times, as was Turkmenistan. A fourth leader, the current president of Tajikistan, is a former cotton farm boss.

The scientists who publicly downplay the disaster may well do so because to criticize old policies would reflect poorly on the country they were raised in and thus on themselves. In my four years of working in education in Central Asia, I sometimes encountered a similar defensive attitude, a lingering sense of "us" versus "them," as if the Cold War were still on.

It's perhaps an innate human characteristic: while we see the Aral Sea vanishing before our eyes, we're blinded by issues of greed, political and personal power, egoism, and insecurity. We become committed to our ideas just as deeply as to our self-preservation, especially those of us whose reputations rely on the acceptance of our ideas, such as politicians, academics, scientists, and writers.

To accept the truth means to accept responsibility, and few people want to do this. It's easier—and frequently more profitable—to keep throwing out the same outdated ideas, half-baked solutions, half-truths, and outright lies. When presented with conviction, these create uncertainty and confusion in the general population, which is inherently disempowering. Too often, this is exactly what those in power want.

⨯

From what I had previously read and learned firsthand on our drive, I had expected the Aral to look like a disaster area, perhaps with chemical slicks pooled on its surface. To be sure, there was at least one evident sign of disaster in the dried-up fish carcasses lining the shore. But aside from that and a few overturned rowboats and skiffs, the sea itself was unqualifiedly beautiful. Its vigorous blue waters stretched before us to the horizon. Puffy cumulus clouds hovered as if painted there, their cotton white tinted with faint suggestions of pink. Gulls wheeled overhead. We walked along the shore, picking up shells and marveling at what we had come so far to see. It was sick, we knew, very sick, but it was still alive. The sickness lay under the surface, invisible, like so many dangers in life.

In a strange way, the tranquility of the scene made it anticlimactic. I hadn't been expecting anything specific, but I'd anticipated something more dramatic. Still, I knew that we were witnessing what many citizens of Aralsk hadn't witnessed in years, some in decades.

"Older people don't go out to see the sea," Agytai explained, "and that's why they think there's no sea left."

We were witnessing what a generation in the region would perhaps never see. We could dip our hands into it, splash them about, feel the salt (and chemical) spray against our faces. As foreigners, we had the means to do so. The four of us together spent the equivalent of a local school teacher's monthly salary just to rent the UAZ. We also had the means to leave the region, to return not only to better parts of Kazakhstan but ultimately to our own homes in the United States. We had access to clean water, healthy food, and good health care whenever we wanted or needed them. We were disaster tourists, slumming it for a time to get a taste of the situation but in no danger of being consumed by it.

I felt self-conscious about this but justified my feelings with the thought that at least the money we spent to get there was going to a local organization trying to save the sea. At least the sandy bread and fruit we bought at the pitiful bazaar was helping, in a small way, the people of Aralsk. And I knew that I would write about this, about them, someday. I may have been a foreigner in the land, but I literally had my hand in the problem now. I had touched the tragedy and in doing so become part of it. Having become part of it, I had no choice but to react in some way. I wanted to be part of a solution.

Today, I'm no longer certain a realistic solution exists, not under the current political conditions. It would take a coordinated effort by all the region's nations to address the issues—the kind of unified approach not seen to date. Study after study indicates that climate change is already affecting the region and will continue to negatively impact it into the future. It is getting hotter and drier. Average temperatures could increase by as much as 2.25 degrees Celsius (up to 2.75 degrees Celsius in summer) by 2050. The mountain glaciers that feed the rivers of the Aral basin—that feed much of Central Asia—are melting and will continue to melt, reducing the amount of water that sustains everything.

In the face of this, the best I can do for now is remember, and by writing down my memories, help others remember not just what was done but exactly how it was done, and why, and by whom.

⁂

It's hard to believe that only sixty years ago, none of this was an issue. The Aral basin ecosystem cohered, thrived in balance. It only took one decision—to grow cotton on an industrial scale in the desert—to wreck the balance and set the entire terrible chain of effects into motion.

Harder still to believe is that some of these effects were foreseen, but the decision was made to proceed anyway.

The Soviet planners in charge of massively expanding irrigation in the 1950s and 1960s expected the Aral Sea to dry up. Scientists had told them this would happen. The planners went ahead with their scheme for one simple reason: they determined that the economic benefits of growing cotton and other agricultural products trumped everything else that the sea could provide.

It has been reported that one Soviet official, swept up in the grand feeling of the enterprise, exclaimed, "The Aral Sea must die, just as a soldier in battle!" This is likely apocryphal, but it nevertheless aptly encapsulates a number of real factors. The planning involved was as precise as any military campaign, with specific objectives and strategies (indeed, the system of Five-Year Plans already in place was perfectly suited for this). Even the name of the overarching project under which all this was mapped out was cast in military jargon: "Virgin Lands Campaign." Previously unbroken ground was to be conquered and seeded. Unlike with most Soviet propaganda, in this case there was no mistaking the language, neither its imagery nor its intended meaning. This was to be nothing short of a war on the Aral, and the Soviets laid siege to it. With supplies cut off, the Aral starved.

Those average citizens who simply hoped to earn a living and raise families became what is euphemistically termed "collateral damage." Such is inevitable in the strange economics of war. It's commonly argued that wars are economically beneficial, but to destroy a country and then build it up again is a waste of resources, both material and human.

Wars may temporarily boost an economy through the production of destructive weapons, but the production of nearly everything useful is curtailed or suspended, one reason why food rationing and famine are common during war.

The human costs—the numbers orphaned, widowed, crippled, maimed, emotionally scarred—are never considered, just as the Soviets never considered conservation in its war against the Aral. A comprehensive plan could have been drawn up that included the building of more efficient canals or crop rotation schedules to reduce nutrient depletion of the soil. The knowledge existed at that time. Local scientists had even invented an anti-infiltration screen that would have substantially reduced water consumption. It was never implemented.

The problem was that the authorities had no incentive—that is, no immediate economic incentive—to be bothered with conservation. They profited richly from waste. The Minvodkhoz (Ministry of Water Management) received billions of rubles for their part in the scheme, this in a time before inflation devalued the ruble; the equivalent in U.S. dollars was also billions.

While it's easy, even comforting, to criticize the Soviets for all this, it's no different from the Ford Motor Company conducting its infamous 1970s analysis that determined it would be more cost-effective to pay off lawsuits over people killed and burned in their lethally flawed Pinto automobiles than to fix the problem (Ford's president then, Lee Iacocca, reportedly often said, "Safety doesn't sell"). It's no different from repeated examples of companies in the twenty-first century—from Enron, Arthur Andersen, and WorldCom to Lehman Brothers, Bernie Madoff, and Satyam Computer Services, and on and on—that have passed off loans as revenue, misstated earnings, and otherwise illegally manipulated their financial records in order to boost corporate bonuses and hide losses, cheating their customers and stealing from their shareholders.

By definition, all are examples of myopia, for the people involved looked at only one aspect of an issue—the bottom line—out of the myriad possible aspects to consider. They also failed to consider the consequences of their decisions.

In the case of the Aral Sea, the planners never foresaw the extreme effects of their decision: the toxic dust storms, the far-ranging desertification, the epidemics of diseases. They never calculated the financial and social costs of poverty, displacement, relocation. They either forgot about or never knew of the stockpiles of biological weapons on Renaissance Island. They had their eyes set on the economic benefits of irrigated farming, and that was all they could see. As Philip Micklin points out in *Science* magazine, "Some optimists even suggested the dried [sea] bottom would be suitable for farming."

In his groundbreaking book *After the Future: The Paradoxes of Postmodernism and Contemporary Russian Culture*, Russian essayist Mikhail Epstein writes,

> And now we can begin to define communist labor not only as the promiscuity of collective ownership, but also as an incestuous attitude toward Mother Nature. Our labor was furious and frenzied, as if we were possessed by insatiable desire. The all-time favorite Soviet saying became the maxim of agronomist Ivan Michurin: "We cannot wait for favors from nature; to take them from her is our task." I remember school teachers constantly repeating this sentence to us with a proud, ardent emphasis on the verb "to take." Labor became a sort of rape: taking by force from Mother Nature those favors she was not inclined to relinquish.

What happened to the Aral wasn't "a sort of" rape. It wasn't metaphorical. It was just as violent and done for the same reasons of power and control.

After us, even flood

And nature stepped away from us
As if we are not needed …
—Osip Mandelstam

I've seen many strange things in my travels through Asia: the Karni Mata Temple in northern India, a holy place packed with thousands of holy rats that scurry up, down, around, and over everything, including visitors' shoes; the Flintstones-like cave cities in Cappadocia, Turkey, carved out of volcanic rock, still inhabited today; the sarcophagus of the Old Testament Prophet Daniel in Uzbekistan, a velvet-draped slab of marble eighteen meters long, for legend says that his body continues to grow. But the sight I saw as the road now opened up in front of us on the Aral's former seabed was the strangest of them all.

There they were, a fleet of ships in the desert.

There were about a dozen in all, rudders jammed into the dry mud, anchors lowered—a redundant gesture. Two large ships, about two hundred feet long and a thousand tons each, stood side by side so close that it was easy to imagine sailors scurrying about to transfer fish or fuel, supplies or crew. The smallest of the group was about one hundred feet long and one hundred tons. It stood alone, an orphan. The others were pointed in every direction as if heedless of their neighbors, a massive traffic jam in the making that was stopped by the receding waters.

"It's a shame these ships were wasted," I said in English. A few minutes later, Agytai said nearly the same thing in Russian.

He explained that as the sea retreated, the fishermen kept moving their fleet to keep it from becoming grounded. Eventually it ended up here, the deepest part. But this became cut off, and the fishermen could do nothing as their ships rode the waters gently to the bottom and then rode the mud that was left until there was no water at all, only baked earth.

Through it all, the ships remained completely upright. From a distance, a mirage shimmering above the sand, they still appeared to be at sea.

"How long have they been here?" I asked Agytai.

"For a long time."

"Exactly how long?"

"A long time," he repeated. He squinted into the past and estimated it had been about thirty years, or since the early 1970s.

We parked the UAZ and walked right up to the beached relics. It was easy enough to climb on board many of them; one featured an open hatch right at ground level, though for most we had to pull ourselves over the gunwales and onto the decks. Anything useful—radios, radar, sounding devices—had been stripped long ago. Even much of the metal had been salvaged as scrap. The rest was left to rust and remember better times.

I plunged down into engine rooms that no longer smelled of diesel but of decay, scurried up ladders on masts where I scouted not schools of fish but rather vistas of desolation. Rusting gangways gave way, imitating the roll and pitch of the sea.

Ordinarily, I'm not a rubbernecker. I don't enjoy watching disasters, either in person or on the news. For some reason, though, I was drawn in fascination to this one. Perhaps it was because it had happened long ago, enough for me to feel removed from it. Perhaps it was because these ships didn't have faces, faded eyes, or raspy, faded voices. Still, they were the ruined relics of real people's livelihoods, and I was crawling all over them as if I were a kid again. I felt a little guilty, but I was having fun. We all were. At the time, it didn't feel like exploitation, but now I'm no longer sure.

⋇

On the way back to Aralsk, our engine died. We were still some thirty kilometers from town, it was already late afternoon, and it had begun to rain. I had visions of a long, wet walk back. Fortunately, Agytai fixed the problem quickly; just as quickly, we became stuck in the sand. Even our four-wheel-drive vehicle could find no traction on the road where there was never meant to be a road. Twice we hopped out and pushed ourselves out of the mire. Eventually it stopped raining, and we found better ground.

Shortly after these incidents, we overtook a man on a bicycle, an old-fashioned model with one gear and high handlebars that forced the rider to sit up straight in his seat. The vision was so absurd that had someone told me it was a mirage I might have believed it, except that we could hear him talking to another man walking alongside him. Where they had come from, and where they were going, was an existential puzzle.

Though the area looked to me no different from what we had just passed through, Agytai became newly animated. He began talking about the spread of the old sea, a place where he swam and camped when he was ten, a beautiful beach with white sands.

"We had a camp there," he said, pointing to a scrubby tree. "Do you see that hill over there? That was the edge of the sea."

Though I consider myself to have a good imagination, I simply could not conjure up the image of how it once looked. The present reality was simply too glaring; it obliterated the thought of everything else. All I could see was a broad, undulating stretch of sand running to a distant bluff and lapping at its base. On the horizon, three camels plowed slowly through this sand-sea.

⁂

Back at the NGO office in Aralsk, hanging almost as an afterthought on a hallway wall, was a painting of the old Aral Sea. Bright blue waters with small whitecaps surged onto a beach so lovely it might have been in the Bahamas or Tahiti. A stout wooden rowboat lay parked there. Behind this, to the left, rose a steep, high bluff topped with a willow tree and thick, soft grasses. The scene was idyllic and inviting, absolutely pristine. One of our party, a local woman, gazed at it for a long moment.

"If that's what it looked like," she finally said, "then the people who ruined it are twice the jerks."

There's a Russian saying, "Posle nas khot potop"—"After us, even flood." It means, "If they won't affect us personally, why should we care about the consequences of our actions?" Say some teenagers enjoy a wild party in somebody's home while the parents are away. When the parents return, those responsible for the destruction will be long gone. *Posle nas khot potop.*

The Soviets had their party. The rest of the world is now aware of all that happened, but there's not much to do about it; the liquor cabinet was raided, the good china broken, and the partygoers dispersed as soon as they heard footsteps on the staircase. We simply have to roll up our sleeves and put our house in order.

Our Aral seas

Whiskey's for drinking; water's for fighting over.
—American folk saying

It's easy for us to feel that the folly of a poorly thought-out and constructed irrigation system and the resulting waste is something that could only happen "over there"—clear proof of failed Soviet ways, and not here in America. In the same way that many Soviet-era scientists and other professionals still feed us their Cold War propaganda, it's clear that many Americans feel our system is inherently superior across the board at all levels.

Yet scarily, many of our practices are every bit as wasteful as those unlined, open canals in Central Asia.

Even in the arid regions that I've lived in, such as southern Idaho and eastern Washington, which average less than twelve inches of precipitation per year, it's common to witness people watering their emerald lawns during the hottest part of a summer's day. Golf courses stand out as lush oases. Houses proliferate in dry, brown foothills, fed by municipal water systems that draw from rivers never meant to spread their reach so far.

Why are we so wasteful? It's as easy to buy a drip irrigation system, which allows water to soak into the ground, as it is to buy a spray system. It's as easy to set a timer to water in the morning and evening, when evaporation is much slower, as it is to set it for the hottest part of the day. Turning off the faucet while brushing one's teeth is easy, saving on average five gallons of water per minute. Installing low-flush toilets and low-flow showerheads pays for itself many times over. Given how Americans love convenience and thrift, it would seem that we would naturally embrace such conservation, which takes little or no effort beyond fitting it in our normal routines and saves us resources and thus money.

But conservation isn't about effort or cost. It's about changing habits. And when confronted with this, people often become defensive. Americans in particular don't like to be told what to do. Only when faced with an emergency do we take the necessary steps to meet it.

We have an emergency.

America has its own Aral Sea. It's called the Ogallala Aquifer.

Based on scale and the number of people that potentially could be affected, the situation with the Ogallala is actually much worse. It underlies approximately two hundred thousand square miles of land, thus covering an area eight times as large as the Aral once did. The aquifer is a major source of fresh water for the arid Great Plains region, a source tapped into by eight states: Colorado, Kansas, Nebraska, New Mexico, Oklahoma, South Dakota, Texas, and Wyoming. A third of all corn grown in the United States is irrigated with water from the Ogallala, and our great "cotton bowl" draws from it as well. It's one of the largest underground water systems in the world. It's also one of the fastest disappearing.

How much water is left varies depending on the section of the aquifer one talks about. In some sections, the water table is dropping three to five feet per year. Some estimates say the entire aquifer may be depleted in only twenty to thirty years. Even the optimists don't give it more than a century if current conditions persist. Either way, there are children being born in the region today who, if they ultimately don't move away as many already have, will likely see their taps run dry, permanently. As with the Aral, the primary reason for the aquifer's disappearance is over-pumping water for irrigation.

There are other parallels. When we hear of how the Soviets considered diverting Siberian rivers thousands of kilometers away to feed the Aral, it sounds like the scheme of some Dr. Strangelove character. Yet we have our own schemes just as grandiose—and potentially catastrophic. Many of these involve building pipelines from the Great Lakes to any number of water-starved regions in our country. Approximately thirty-four million people, or 9 percent of the combined populations of the United States and Canada, live in the Great Lakes basin and rely on its waters. To pipe water out of this basin would put this huge number of people at risk of serious water shortages. The Great Lakes hold approximately 20 percent of the world's surface freshwater and a staggering 90 percent of North America's, yet they recharge at the rate of only 1 percent per year. This is primarily due to their small watershed; while they cover an enormous amount of land, they drain a relatively small portion. Should they begin shrinking, less evaporation would result in a drier surrounding climate, decreasing rainfall and thus decreasing another source of the lakes' recharge, exacerbating the problem.

This would be exactly what happened to the Aral Sea. Yet while the majority of scientists are adamantly against any pipeline plans, the idea is often bandied about by politicians and others as a solution to water problems in other parts of the United States, mostly the desert West. Demands for water are particularly high in our most populous state, California, where a number of lakes have disappeared or are disappearing.

One of the most famous examples is Owens Lake. It was drained within a period of twenty years in the early part of the twentieth century when the City of Los Angeles—led by a corrupt mayor and a cadre of ruthless businessmen using deceit and bribery—diverted water from the Owens Valley, a story that in part inspired the 1974 film *Chinatown*. But the lake is far from being a historical footnote. Today, dust containing toxic elements such as arsenic and cadmium is blown from the dry lakebed in fierce storms throughout the valley and beyond. It's the largest point source of particle pollution in the country. The only viable solution was to flood the lakebed shallowly and plant native salt grasses to keep the dust down, which cost more than four hundred million dollars to set up and requires more than forty million dollars a year in water to maintain. The total cost to date has been more than two billion dollars.

Then there's the Salton Sea. Over the past two decades, as the lake level has fallen and its waters have grown increasingly salinized, 97 percent of its former population of one hundred million fish have died, a story similar to the Aral's. Only in this case, San Diego is to blame for sucking the water sources away. Some people feel this sea isn't worth saving. After all, its current form dates to only a century ago, when a canal breeched and sent the Colorado River spilling into the Salton Sink. But should the Salton dry up, it will result in dust storms full of pesticides, salts, and heavy metals, as at Owens Lake, only the exposed area would be more than three times larger.

The projected reclamation cost? Up to one billion dollars, and that to save but a portion of the sea.

Like the Soviets, we justify our environmentally destructive decisions in the name of economics. But when faced with the price of cleanup, which often runs into the hundreds of millions of dollars, it becomes clear that even economically our decisions are unsound. Ultimately, we pay. The issue is really over who profits in the short term. Environmental destruction is systemic, part of our way of life and doing business, but it's a system that benefits a relatively few wealthy people at the expense of the vast majority. It's devilishly clever in how it moves money around. The public pays in several ways. We pay in taxes that subsidize many companies or in the loss of tax income when these companies are given special incentives. We pay for their products. We pay in absorbing the ill effects of their production. Finally, we pay for the cleanup.

※

While the U.S. enjoys some of the world's lowest gasoline prices, many Americans bemoan the slightest increase at the pumps (I know people who will wait for an hour or more in long lines to save ten cents a gallon), and yet they don't seem to think anything of paying $1.69 for a liter of bottled water—not Perrier, not even generic mineral water, but just plain, filtered water in a bottle. Often it's simply municipal tap water in pretty packaging. Yet that price translates to an astounding $6.40 a gallon, more than double the price of gas. In some markets, bottled water sells for up to $10 a gallon.

Americans drank 14.4 billion gallons in 2019, according to industry figures, more than any other category of beverage, even though it's often not any healthier than tap water and can cost anywhere from two thousand to ten thousand times more. The majority of bottled water is sold in single-serve polyethylene terephthalate (PET) bottles, helping plastic account for almost half of all beverage packaging. When did it happen that a resource that constitutes 70 percent of our bodies, that we die from lack of after only seven days, that surrounds us in oceans, lakes, rivers, glaciers, clouds, and the tissues of every living thing, became such an expensive and environmentally harmful commodity?

It's analogous to the situation in the Aral Sea region. The people there were told to grow cotton, and they came to rely on the cash from that crop to pay for basic food necessities they once grew themselves for a fraction of the cost. We, too, have done exactly what we were told to do—build our factories, log our forests, mine our mountains, and irrigate our farms—and we came to rely on the cash from these activities to buy the very resource we once enjoyed for free, before our activities polluted it and made it scarcer.

Everywhere on the planet, it's the same. The United Nations World Water Development Report 2020 estimates that four billion people, or more than half of the world's population, live in areas of severe water scarcity at least one month per year. By 2050, this figure could run as high as almost six billion people. As former French President Jacques Chirac prophetically suggested at the 2003 World Water Forum, this century could be a time of "tension and water wars." Or to use the old American folk saying, "Whiskey's for drinking; water's for fighting over."

The BBC has identified twelve water "hot spots." These include the Aral Sea and the Ogallala Aquifer. Two hot spots, Israel and Iraq, are ravaged by war. Others are in countries with tremendously high, dense urban populations, such as Mexico, India, and China, exemplifying how it's impossible to talk about water shortages—or environmental pressures of any kind—without talking about the exploding human population and unsustainable economic development.

In China, an estimated 360 million people—or more than the entire population of the United States—live in rural regions that lack potable water. In a country that's more than a quarter desert, with as little as 7 percent of the planet's fresh water but almost 20 percent of the population, this problem is certain to grow worse.

Their answer? Work is already well underway on a massive diversion project to bring water thousands of kilometers from the monsoon-soaked south to Beijing and other dry northern cities. It's the largest such project ever undertaken.

Recent gains—or are they?

In every drop of water, there is a grain of gold.
—Uzbek proverb

The $85.8 million joint Kazakhstan–World Bank project to revive the Northern Aral Sea is showing results well ahead of schedule. A new dam prevents water from draining into the Southern Aral, while improved waterworks along the Syr Darya allow more water to flow into the Northern Aral. This resulted in the water level rising three meters within seven months, much more quickly than the five to ten years experts had expected. Already nearly a thousand square kilometers of dried seabed have been reclaimed, and the region's climate is changing. Clouds are coming back, as are the rains. Fish—and not just salt-resistant flounder but also pike, carp, and bream among more than a dozen species—are being caught again, though the waters still don't reach the old ports; the fishermen must drive every morning to the sea. But it's closer. Old villagers who thought they would never see the sea again now weep at the prospect of doing so. The out-migration of people from the region has slowed considerably, and some have even returned. The standard of living is slowly rising.

It's all so encouraging that the government of Kazakhstan began negotiating with the World Bank for money to implement a second phase of the restoration project to raise the dam another six meters, which could bring the waters tantalizingly close to Aralsk. These plans have stalled, and it's uncertain when they will gain traction again. Meanwhile, there are fears the dam could collapse, stressed to its limits at its current size.

Despite such concerns, there has been much congratulatory talk about the overall success of the project, as there should be. But the Northern Aral is also called the Little Aral for a reason. Too often overlooked is that the Southern Aral—the much larger portion, and the portion suffering most severely—is doomed to be lost to evaporation. This oversight has led to some pronouncements that would be humorous if they didn't ultimately reveal the continuing effects of the disaster and the underlying biases that shape judgments and analyses of it.

"World Bank restores Aral Sea" boldly proclaims the headline to an article in *The Washington Times* dated April 1, 2006. The timing of publication was fitting, for the headline was highly deceiving. The article actually referred to the project expected to revive the Little Aral, not the entire sea.

The Little Aral represents but a fraction of the Aral's former size, and only two-thirds of this smaller sea is expected to be saved, provided that Kazakhstan follows through properly on the second phase of its collaboration with the World Bank. A projection made at the beginning of the first phase estimated that the Little Aral would stabilize at 3,500 square kilometers, or roughly 5 percent of the area the Aral formerly covered. Yet the article enthuses, "It would achieve one of biggest reversals of an environmental disaster in history." The writer appears to have overlooked 95 percent of the sea when he wrote that.

A decade and a half later, even as the earlier modest estimates haven't been met, the press remains enthusiastic in overselling the achievement. "The country that brought a sea back to life" trumpets the headline to a July 22, 2018, article from the BBC, though the Little Aral covers only around 3,000 square kilometers.

While saving the Little Aral is a desirable goal, one worth the effort and something to build upon, it's difficult to understand how saving less than 5 percent of anything can deserve any more than muted enthusiasm. Aralsk may once again enjoy some measure of its old prosperity, but Muynak, the former fishing port in Uzbekistan that once rivaled Aralsk, will likely never be revived. And no one is claiming that the noxious dust storms will entirely cease, that the region's climate will be fully restored, or that the health problems of its people will dramatically improve overnight.

Both articles, with their focus on the World Bank, also show our persistent bias that any problem can be solved as long as we throw enough money at it. Even more revealing, *The Washington Times* headline suggests that the World Bank alone is responsible for whatever gains have been made regarding the Little Aral. The Kazakhstani people, who have been gamely dealing with the mess for decades, are relegated to the role of bit players.

A September 28, 2005, article in the *International Herald Tribune* reveals another persistent belief, one almost religious in nature: that of technology as savior. In that article, Russian Aral Sea specialist Nikolai Aladin is quoted as rejoicing, "What man has destroyed, man can now restore."

Superficially, this sounds poetic, hopeful, even life-affirming, a statement of humanity's desire to do more good than harm. Looked at more deeply, it reveals one of our greatest troubles: poor moral development paired with a science-fiction perception of science.

There's nothing inherently bad about science. Neither is there anything inherently good. It's simply a tool. To be used effectively, it must be matched with good judgment. This would seem to be so obvious as to be commonsensical. Yet repeatedly, all over the world, we plunge ahead with our technological plans even when those plans have grave flaws because we believe that time will ultimately produce better technology to fix those flaws. For example, given the half-life of radioactive isotopes, all current nuclear waste containment sites are temporary, but we continue to bury nuclear waste in the belief that we will build better containment sites. Someday.

This uncritical belief that our science and technology can fix anything is arrogant, and to call it anything less is to fail to accept responsibility for our actions. Rather than working continually in crisis mode to fix our problems, we should learn how to avoid making those problems in the first place.

For the most part, however, we go about our business as usual and worry about the consequences later. This is an immature and irresponsible attitude. As adults, we should understand the value of review and the wisdom of planning—the subtle back-and-forth of learning from the past and looking into the future that keeps us properly focused on the present. Yet we continue to abuse the environment and then scramble madly to soothe it, all the while castigating ourselves for knowing better, the behavior of addicts or fetishists. We flagellate ourselves to atone for our sins and then say that we deserved it. We're masochists, and I don't use this word lightly. Gratifying ourselves with short-term economic pleasure and self-congratulatory technological boasts at the cost of long-term devastation and pain is nothing short of masochism.

Our behavior toward the earth can properly be called sadistic. We think little of harming it because it appears to be inert and thus immune to harm, a ball of dust that only through our prodding intervention can be coaxed into providing what we desire. Yet it's our home as surely as any four walls that shelter us.

As we have diligently sought to understand the Aral's disappearance, so we must also diligently seek to understand our behavior. These are linked as intimately as hydrogen and oxygen in every molecule of water. But while much emphasis has been put on what it might take to save the Aral—more money, better dam projects, improved irrigation technologies—I've only read hints of the most fundamental part of the solution: a complete change in our attitude toward nature.

⁜

Some decisions in life are small, such as deciding to hit the snooze button and sleep for five more minutes. Some are large, such as choosing whom to marry. All have consequences, and these consequences require us to make more decisions, leading to an interlinked chain of events that can appear to be the will of fate. There are those who would argue that economic and political circumstances determine our decisions, that the pressures Soviet planners faced were too great for them to act according to their consciences. Even if true, it doesn't negate the decisions. Economic conditions and political pressures are not causes for morally unsound actions. They are factors. As such, they need to be considered, but not at the expense of considering the full range of factors that shape an issue.

In my research for this, I encountered streams of facts and statistics—a flow that if it were water might save the Aral. These are important to know, and I've gathered many of them here. However, no matter how assiduously this information was researched and presented, and no matter how damning it may be, it conspicuously stands in absence of any direct condemnations of the scientists, planners, and politicians for the weak moral foundation that gave rise to their actions.

Facts and statistics are only ways of reckoning the *effects* of the disaster, not its causes. Admittedly, the causes in many ways cannot be reckoned because they directly relate to our human nature, which inherently cannot be enumerated. Because it's so complex and resists enumeration, that might explain why so few scientists and writers have been willing to explore it. Grigory Reznichenko hinted at it when describing the difficulties he experienced in finding a publisher for his book: "Party leaders in Russia and the Central Asian republics were and are sickened by glasnost, even though they introduced it, for it reveals the unseemly actions of the powers that be, their plundering attitude toward nature, the barbaric destruction of its resources." I will be more direct: these men (and the principal players were all men) lacked even the moderate sense of moral values that could have prevented the disaster. They lacked integrity.

According to *Merriam-Webster's Unabridged Dictionary*, one of the definitions of integrity is "avoidance of deception, expediency, artificiality, or shallowness of any kind." The last element in that list reads like a bad pun, but there's no doubt that had the Soviet planners possessed integrity, they could have avoided the shallowness of today's Aral Sea.

Anyone who uses words such as "integrity" runs the risk of moralizing, or at least of being accused of moralizing, but there's much greater risk in not facing such issues honestly. Moreover, it would be cowardly. It's not easy to develop a sense of responsibility and act on it. But we have seen ad nauseum—literally, to the point of physical sickness—the results of people taking the easy way.

⁂

Would the Aral have dried up on its own again someday? Likely, yes—in a few thousand years. But humans have catastrophically sped up the process; mapmakers can hardly keep up with the changes. The local flora and fauna have had no time to adjust, perhaps to adapt or migrate to other areas.

Nor have the local people.

Activities that lack balance reflect the unbalanced nature of those performing them. That we prize economic benefits above all others is unbalanced. That we seek short-term over long-term gains is unbalanced. That we put our full faith in technology rather than in natural systems is unbalanced. This is not indicative of a healthy species. Earning an adequate income is necessary, but maintaining strong family and community ties and a respectful relationship with our surroundings is equally important and costs nothing. To use technology consciously and conscientiously can be useful, but to continue willfully pursuing activities that are unsustainable reflects a deep-seated aggression, not only against the environment but also against ourselves. *When we try to pick out anything by itself, we find it hitched to everything else in the Universe.*

Humans have been engineering the environment for millennia, and we will continue to do so. Many, including me, would argue that this is as natural as any act any creature makes in this world. But to what degree do we have a right to do this? Do economic needs justify actions that help feed and clothe us even as they destroy the environment? Do we take priority over all other living things?

There must be limits. Difficult circumstances don't absolve us from our moral responsibilities, from taking a long-term, balanced view in which human interests are weighed equally with the interests of other animals and the plants, water, and air they need to survive. In the end, we need these to survive as well, as the Aral disaster makes painfully clear.

Facing our choices

Nothing is farther away than yesterday; nothing is closer than tomorrow.
—Kazakh proverb

Many of those writing about the Aral Sea lament the massive amounts of chemicals blown from the dry seabed, but precious few lament that these chemicals were used in the first place. Others are troubled that the stockpiles of biological weapons on Renaissance Island may fall into the wrong hands, but I've encountered none who seem troubled that these weapons were made or who even question their need. Apparently, it's a given for most scientists and journalists that agriculture and synthetic chemicals go together as naturally as air and water, that bioweapons are to humans as babies are to their mothers. We rarely question these assumptions in the name of "being realistic," but nothing will change until we choose to face the contradictions in what we've been trained to believe.

The large-scale industrial model of farming isn't inherently more viable than traditional or progressive methods, not in all circumstances. Yet Americans are told that we need the agribusiness model in order to be more productive, even though we're already so productive that we grow more food than we can eat or export, and the government pays farmers subsidies not to grow more food.

The creation of inhuman tools of butchery doesn't arise out of inevitable need. A biological weapon can never feed, house, or clothe us, can never offer us condolence, wisdom, or hope. It has one purpose: to kill in a widespread, efficient, and psychologically terrifying way. Yet when these weapons are accidentally released into the environment or tested on humans—as they inevitably are—we're repeatedly surprised at the results. We're concerned about the bioweapons on Renaissance Island only because we fear that terrorists might find and use them; we expect large industrialized countries to manufacture such weapons. We're told that they provide security. But can we truly maintain security with them if we must constantly worry about that security being breeched?

Today, we have access to more information than at any other time in the world's history. This makes it imperative that we know how to use that information better and more wisely than ever.

Truth exists. Facts matter. Honesty and integrity still have meaning. A curious attitude guided by sound reasoning and disciplined action balanced with compassion still produces the best results. We can't be swayed into questioning all this. We can't allow ourselves to be gaslighted by those who want to obfuscate the facts for their own personal or political gain over the good of the majority.

We're living in an age when doublespeak is threatening the integrity of our language as never before, and this threatens the integrity of our very selves. As surely as we shape language, so does language shape us. We cannot make statements such as "science has not determined the cause of global warming" without feeling its ambivalence, becoming the confusion itself, even as polar ice caps melt, average temperatures continue rising, and hotter and more massive wildfires destroy more acres of forests than in recorded history, all as predicted by scientists and also all frighteningly ahead of the predicted schedule. We cannot praise the economic benefits of ecologically devastating practices without coming to believe our own words that indeed the greatest profits provide us with the greatest benefits, even as other benefits such as clean water, clean air, fertile soils, and healthy communities disappear, unenumerated, before our eyes. Without understanding that what we say and believe is connected to what we do, consequences tend to look like cruel accidents, twists of fate, the whims of God. They are not.

The Aral Sea disaster wasn't inevitable, nor were the current crises that loom before us: the falling Ogallala Aquifer, our disappearing lakes, water wars, global warming, or even the overarching issue of climate change. While we are already beyond the point of avoiding these crises completely, their worst effects can still be mitigated, though only if we take immediate and radical action by completely restructuring the way we interact with our environment, with our neighbors, and with ourselves. Conservation is not a new idea. Neither is cooperation between nations. We have all the tools we need. Human ingenuity and creativity are boundless. If we took a fraction of the energy that we currently use to create weapons and fight wars and instead invested it in constructive projects—building new water purification and desalination plants; improving existing water treatment and sanitation systems, especially their ability to recycle wastewater, and investing in renewable energy sources to power them; improving water harvesting technologies; and developing better distribution infrastructure—we would go a long way toward ensuring a clean supply of water for all with enough profit to keep everyone happy.

We must begin to calculate the true cost of our actions now. This requires thinking much more broadly and long-term than we ever have before. It also involves asking tough questions. They are tough not because they are complex but rather because they are broad, and addressing them requires broad consensus, coordination, and cooperation among all the many elements of society—the hardest kind of work but the most essential in any democracy:

Why are we not more mindful of conserving water? Of conserving all our natural resources? Can we in good conscience continue to buy cotton or any other products from countries that engage in socially exploitive and environmentally destructive practices? Shouldn't we use our economic influence to foster positive change rather than isolating ourselves from the world around us? Shouldn't we change our own destructive practices while we still have a chance to change the course of events, before they bloom into irrevocable crises? Why keep putting off doing what we ultimately must do if we as a species are to survive?

We don't have any more time. We do have a choice.

The Technicolor mural in the train station in Aralsk could be a blueprint of how humans can come together to help each other when the call is made.

Or the image of ships riding the sands could end up representing more than poor Soviet planning and a disaster in a relatively sparsely populated region of the world. It could become a metaphor for our own lives.

THE MISSIONARY POSITION

A Personal Exploration of the Politics of Persuasion in Central Asia

During my first summer in Kazakhstan, I woke up early every morning to the sounds of my village: roosters crowing, dogs barking, cows lowing while sauntering to their mountain pastures, the sharp smack of the pastukh's stick against their thick hides. I was already on my way to gaining an astonishing twenty pounds (which thankfully I later lost) from being so assiduously attended to by my host mother, Farida; breakfast usually consisted of soup, meat, or noodles left over from dinner the night before, several eggs, something sweet, and in the Kazakhstani style, a pot of tea and plenty tandoor-baked lepyoshka bread. At 7:30 I would begin my half-hour walk uphill to the private home where three of my fellow Peace Corps trainees and I studied Russian every Monday through Friday. The lush green foothills fronting the perennially snow-peaked Tian Shan range formed a daily feast for my vision, but if it had rained recently, which it often did that summer, the narrow, winding dirt roads would turn into streams of mud. In dry weather the path was so rough that I wore out the soles of a good pair of shoes.

On the way, I passed the village school, a mere five minutes from my home. We had been hiking to our lessons for some time before we learned why we had to go so far instead of studying in the nearby school as the trainees in other villages did. Our school's director thought we were missionaries. As a Muslim, he'd had a bad experience with a group of Korean Christian missionaries a few years before, and though we never found out exactly what had happened, it had affected him so deeply that he refused to work with us no matter how often and strenuously our Peace Corps Russian instructor explained that we were *teachers*, not missionaries.

Later, during my two years as a volunteer university instructor in the southern city of Shymkent, I came to partially understand the director's position. Most missionaries, particularly Christians, come to Central Asia in the guise of teachers. A few are open about their real intentions. The rest are, to varying degrees, secretive. The reason for this is simple: in a region that is primarily Muslim, they are often seen as dangerous influences on or, at the very worst, outright corrupters of the predominant culture.

It was in this time that Kyrgyzstani authorities issued a decree stating that groups outside of Central Asia's two mainstream religions, Islam and Russian Orthodoxy, are "totalitarian sects … using deceptions, silent methods and obtrusive propaganda in order to attract new members." A contemporaneous analysis of Kazakhstani nationalist newspapers reveals an even more acid attitude toward missionaries, often portraying them as preying upon the young. In this analysis, "Perceptions of Threats from 'Alien Faiths,'" which appeared in *Central Asia and Islam*, William Fierman writes, "According to one article, a Christian church was placed next to a Kazakh school specifically because there it would be convenient to 'cast a hook to children.'" In another instance, "The Kazakh members of one Evangelist congregation in Almaty are said to be primarily 'girls who just yesterday wearing the white ribbons of their childhood in their hair came to the city seeking to fulfill their dreams.'"

The more recent rise in Islamic fundamentalism around the world and an attendant Central Asian fear of this has even made many Muslims suspect. Today in Kazakhstan, there are restrictions on Muslims from outside the particular school of Sunni Islam that the government considers traditional to the region. Those who wear conservative clothing such as headscarves are sometimes discriminated against. All missionaries regardless of their religion or nationality are required to be registered by the state, though simply speaking to others about one's faith or posting religious quotes online can result in fines or even imprisonment, as the U.S. Office of International Religious Freedom has noted in its series of reports over the past two decades. Directly before I first arrived in the country, after a trial that had lasted nearly two years, two Muslim teachers from Saudi Arabia were expelled for "fomenting national and religious hostility among the peoples of Kazakhstan." One newspaper reflecting on this issue wrote, "Missionaries come and go, but they do not always bear good promises and charity."

The word "missionary" derives from the Latin verb mittere, "to send off," and originally meant "someone sent with a message." But in today's world it has come to carry many other shades of meaning, none of them neutral, only a few of them good. Where exactly is the line between sending someone with a message and outright cultural imperialism? And why, in a region that has for more than two thousand years been a melting pot of religions and cultures, a meeting place between East and West, should any religious idea, however new, be seen as a threat?

On top of all that, am I not a missionary in many ways, preaching, no matter how secularly or subtly, my own cultural values? In that sense, isn't everyone a missionary?

Ultimately, this essay may be about my belief in the freedom of each individual to choose his or her own values, about the silk-fine line that separates the democratic religious pluralism that makes true choice possible from the mere presence of various religions, each intent on proselytizing.

A non-denominational Congregational upbringing

My interest in missionaries stems from my earliest serious questioning of the Christian church when I was thirteen or fourteen. I was born into a moderately religious Midwestern family and attended regular services, Sunday school, and events such as Vacation Bible School from the time of my earliest memories. When told that the church where I spent most of my childhood was "non-denominational congregational," I first heard a little "c," but when I later learned that its official name, the First Congregational Church, denoted a specific denomination, I became confused. It was just one of many inconsistencies I would encounter.

Along with my puberty bloomed a sense of intellectual curiosity. To reconcile what I saw as difficulties in the Bible, I typed a two-page list of questions that I presented to my pastor. Included was a question about why people of other faiths should be destined to Hell when, it seemed to me, it was by random fate they were born into non-Christian cultures. He answered that "all will hear the word of God," as proof quoting Jesus in John 6:45: "It is written in the Prophets: 'They will all be taught by God.' Everyone who listens to the Father and learns from him comes to me." But realistically, many could never expect to hear the Christian word of God, I returned. What of peoples living behind inaccessible mountain ranges or deep within remote deserts? My pastor's reply was to repeat the verse and say that it was the truth because the Bible said so and the Bible was the word of God.

Though I didn't have a name for it then, I understood that his answer was a logical fallacy—"begging the question," as I would later explain in my critical thinking classes in Shymkent, or circular logic. His answer struck me as being stubbornly simpleminded.

But perhaps there was more to it than that. His faith in the Christian word of God reaching all the earth's inhabitants may have stemmed not only from his ironclad belief in the infallibility of the

Bible but equally from the knowledge that Christian missionaries were penetrating remote mountain and desert regions even as we spoke—though then, with the Iron Curtain firmly in place and glasnost still around the corner, Soviet Central Asia was not among those regions.

More disturbing to me was that my pastor didn't seem to respect non-Christian cultures enough to leave them alone. Though I grew up within the Christian church, I somehow never came to view it as the only path, or even the best among many. From an early age, I was fascinated by other time periods and cultures, particularly Native Americans and the Mongol hordes of Genghis Khan. My best friends might as well have been my family's 1950s eighteen-volume *The World Book Encyclopedia* and our collection of *National Geographic* magazines, which I poured over repeatedly. In the former, I knew exactly where the multi-page color section on North American native tribes lay (under "I" for "Indian," the term in use then) and the section on world alphabets with a beautiful example of Arabic script I found so entrancing that I created my own alphabet imitating the flowing lines, loops, and diamond-shaped dots.

Twenty-five years later, on a fifteen-hour train ride to Almaty, Kazakhstan, I would find myself sharing a kupe compartment with a Muslim Uzbek family—a grandfather, his daughter, and her son. They were from Tashkent, Uzbekistan's capital, only two hours from my home, then in Shymkent. The Uzbekistani government, while an ally of the U.S. in the so-called war on terror, is recognized around the world for its shocking human rights abuses; theirs is a country where just wearing a beard and regularly attending mosque can get one thrown in jail for years as a suspected Muslim militant. This grandfather was a teacher, dressed conservatively in a suit, clearly loving of his daughter and grandson, whom he watched over with the greatest care. Even with my middling Russian, I could understand him. He wasn't an insurgent; he didn't even talk about deep political issues. He simply spoke in the broad, passionate way of one whose voice had been bottled up for too long, about the things that matter to him in his life: a decent salary, the price of tomatoes, the freedom to speak his mind.

Listening to him for much of the evening as our train climbed through the Talassky Alatau range, leaving Uzbekistan behind, I realized he could say none of these things in his home country and had probably been saving them all up for this train ride. I have come to understand that his need for a voice, for an outlet to express who he was, is representative of many in the region. After seventy years of Soviet rule on top of many previous decades of Tsarist repression, Central Asians are now seeking their own identity, something indigenous, something that represents the spirit of who they are and where they come from. It is into this context of not just nation-building but culture-building that today's missionaries come, and this is a big reason why they often cause such controversy.

Silk Road Central Asia and the Golden Age of Islam

What exactly is at stake in Central Asia? And how does it relate more broadly to the rest of the world? To understand this, we first must look at some history. The region has a spectacularly rich past that surprisingly few in the West know about, and it is worth examining in some detail here.

While Central Asia is crossed by some of the world's highest mountain ranges and most forbidding deserts, its broad grasslands attracted a number of nomadic empires over the centuries, including the famed Scythians and infamous Huns. More importantly, in the age before global sea power, its strategic location between the rich Chinese and Indian states and those of Asia Minor made it critically important to trade. In approximately the second century B.C., the first of what became a network of overland caravan routes was formed, which ultimately linked ancient East with West. Today this is known as the Great Silk Road. At its greatest, this network stretched from the Pacific to the Mediterranean and from the Indian plains to beyond the Ural Mountains. Its longest and most dangerous sections passed through Central Asia.

Vast quantities of goods were traded along this "road," including spices, jewels and semi-precious stones, Byzantine glass, Chinese porcelain and paper, Persian carpets, horses (the "heavenly horses" of Central Asia were especially prized), tea, rice, furs, and, of course, silk. But physical goods formed only part of the trade. The cosmopolitan caravan cities that sprang up along the Silk Road's various branches also saw the exchange of music and musicians, arts and artists, languages and literature, sports, customs, clothing, even hairstyles.

Central Asia was already financially and culturally prosperous by the time of the Muslim Arab invasion in the early eighth century A.D., but it gained a new strength after that. This period, which lasted until sea trade began obsoleting the Silk Road in the sixteenth century, might properly be called the Golden Age of Islam. While Christian Europe struggled through the Middle Ages, Islamic Central Asia flourished. Its cities were like names in a fairytale—Kashgar, Samarkand, Bukhara, Khiva, Merv—conjuring up all the color, intrigue, and romance of *The Arabian Nights*. Samarkand in particular enjoyed prominence for a thousand years; its population peaked at 150,000 during the fourteenth and fifteenth centuries, far outstripping Moscow, London, and Paris at that time. Samarkand's palaces and gardens were said to have inspired envy even in the two greatest cities west of China, Cairo and Baghdad.

Central Asia was a world leader in everything from politics to architecture, the arts to the sciences. Its medressas, or Islamic universities, trained some of the best and most influential minds of the time: Abu Nasr al-Farabi, known as the "Second Master" after Aristotle, a philosopher, logician, musician, and political scientist who left behind major written works in each of these disciplines and made important contributions to mathematics, science, psychology, and sociology as well; Muhammad ibn Musa al-Khwarizmi, who devised the concepts of algorithms and algebra in the ninth century; Abu

Raihan Muhammad al-Biruni, who knew that the earth rotated on its axis around the sun, calculating its distance to the moon within an astounding twenty kilometers—more than four centuries before Columbus sailed; Abu Ali ibn Sina (known in the West as Avicenna), who in the eleventh century wrote his *Canon of Medicine*, a standard textbook for Western doctors until the seventeenth century.

There is a Greek word, also used by the Christian saint Augustine—eudaimonia—which means "human flourishing." In many ways, it was a unique time and place in human history for eudaimonia.

Yet there is danger in idealizing anything, particularly the past. To be sure, the Golden Age was also a time of repeated invasions and strict autocratic rule. Many Muslim rulers then were corrupt and cruel, and while there was a substantial middle class of merchants and traders, democracy as we know it today was nonexistent. Women's rights were nonexistent. Slavery still flourished, as it did everywhere else in the world at the time. All this must be acknowledged. The Golden Age was not perfect and is not an ideal to aim for. It provides not a blueprint but rather an outline to a possible new beginning, a suggestion of what might be built upon and improved.

Its most impressive achievement may be that in Silk Road Central Asia, spiritual and humanistic knowledge were arguably as thoroughly integrated as in any culture before or since. Theologians and scientists both could freely and openly investigate the universe around them. The region was, as it still is, a stronghold of Sufism, the mystical branch of Islam known for its stress on gnosis—literally Greek for "knowledge," more specifically the inner and inexpressible knowledge gained from direct experience with the divine. Featuring much less control by central authorities than most religions with its emphasis on the individual nature of the adherent's search for God, Sufism was perfectly suited to the intellectual classes as well as the highly independent traders and nomads of the region.

Sufism also melded well with the various shamanic belief systems held by the native peoples. By the tenth century, most of the region's population had converted to Islam, though many of the old customs prevailed and were absorbed into the new religion, forming what has been described as a type of syncretic folk Islam.

For example, female shamans have always been greatly respected as healers in traditional society. This view was simply carried over and adapted in Central Asia. Women there continue to enjoy more highly visible roles in religious life than in more orthodox countries. Sufis were not the first missionaries in Central Asia, nor would they be the last, but they left a lasting impression.

Probably the most famous is Jalal al-Din Rumi (b. 1207). Though most well-known as the founder of the Mevlevi whirling dervish order in Turkey, he spent the first thirteen years of his life in Balkh in Afghan Turkestan, present-day north Afghanistan. His ecstatic religious poetry, of which two brief excerpts from his *Mathnavi* are below, is universally recognized for the depth of its insight and emotion:

> Every prophet has received from Him the guarantee:
> Seek help with patience and prayer.
> Come, ask of Him, not anyone except Him.
> Seek water in the sea; do not seek it in the dry river bed.

and

> What is unification?
> To burn one's self before the One.

⁂

This is the social, political, scientific, artistic, and spiritual heritage that rightly belongs to every Muslim in Central Asia.

But is it that simple?

Islam has long been the strongest religion in the region, but it was a relative latecomer to the scene; for the first thousand years of the Silk Road, Buddhism was the predominant religion. And Christianity, while always playing a minority role, has been around nearly from its beginning and exerted more influence than many today realize.

From its inception as a few isolated routes into unknown lands, the Silk Road was a combination of both trade and missionary efforts. Buddhism arrived in Central Asia on the Silk Road's very first branches, and it remained until Genghis Khan's rout of the region put all aspects of life on hold; in the second flowering of culture that rose from the ashes, Buddhism was left behind.

But in the millennium and a half in-between those events, at least three major Buddhist sects—Shravakayana, Vajrayana, and Tibetan Buddhism—all found favor at different times and in different localities in Central Asia. The Chinese pilgrim Fa-hien or Faxian, who journeyed through the region from 399 to 413 A.D., wrote of the Silk Road city-state of Khotan, "The country is prosperous and the people are numerous; without exception they have faith in the Dharma [the Buddhist principle or law that orders the universe] and they entertain one another with religious music. The community of monks numbers several tens of thousands. …"

At the same time, coming from the other direction, Christianity was flexing its own missionary muscles. By the Middle Ages, even Samarkand, a city clothed in such powerful Muslim mythology, had been feeling the effects of this "foreign" religion for centuries. In the early fifteenth century the Spanish envoy Ruy González de Clavijo reported the presence of many Christians there, including Greeks and Armenians, Catholics, Jacobites, and Nestorians.

A cornucopia of religions

All creatures are God's children, and those dearest to God are the ones who treat His children kindly.

—From the Ahadith, or the collected sayings and deeds of the Prophet Muhammad

To make matters even more interesting, Islam, Buddhism, and Christianity were just three in a cornucopia of religions that mingled and flourished together during the nearly two millennia of the Silk Road in Central Asia, along with Judaism, Manichaeism, and Zoroastrianism from the West, Confucianism and Taoism from the East, and countless variations of local animistic, shamanistic religions.

Travelers from various cultures noted the religious tolerance of the region during this time, particularly during the reign of the Mongol empire from their conquest of Samarkand to Tamerlane's establishment of a capital there (1220–1370), for the bloody but culture-loving Mongols promoted a policy of tolerance. In his essay "The Pax Mongolica," Central Asian scholar Daniel Waugh notes, "Marco Polo, for one, emphasized the apparent willingness of [Mongol emperor] Qubilai Khan to entertain all the 'religions of the book,'" and that "Mongol rule witnessed a revival in Nestorian Christianity throughout Eurasia, the spread of Tibetan Buddhism through China to Mongolia, and the expansion of Islam in areas of Eastern Europe." In describing how the Mongols' famously efficient postal relay system helped "favored travelers," Waugh enthuses, "We cannot but be impressed by the ability of defenseless Franciscans to travel across most of Eurasia in the middle of the thirteenth century."

During the Golden Age of Islam, such religious tolerance was the norm, not just in Central Asia but in the entire Islamic world. Historian and professor James Loewen writes in *Lies My Teacher Told Me* that today's college students are often "astonished to learn that Turks and Moors allowed Jews and Christians freedom of worship at a time when European Christians tortured or expelled Jews and Muslims." (The sections on Islam and Islamic history cover only a handful of pages, but in general I recommend this book to anyone interested in learning how American thinking has been shaped by falsehoods that are perpetuated largely for unstated reasons of cultural and religious imperialism.) This is in complete contrast to the unfortunate view held by too many Westerners that all Muslims are backward, vaguely threatening fundamentalists or worse.

Civilizations have risen and fallen and sometimes risen again in Central Asia. It has always been a crossing grounds, a melting pot. It is impossible to speak of definitively, only in broad trends. But history allows us to see these trends, and they have something very important to teach us if only we might look closely enough. For the period of greatest flourishing of Islam in Central Asia coincides exactly with the period of greatest religious efflorescence. And the end of this Golden Age corresponds both with the end of the Silk Road as the world's most important economic highway and the end of this religious efflorescence.

Conventional wisdom tells us that culture can only develop when people have time and freedom from material constraints. By this reasoning, Silk Road Central Asia was so cultured and tolerant because it was so prosperous; people had the money and leisure to develop culture and no need to compete with each other over the ideas of religion.

I feel, as others may, that it worked the other way, too—the religious tolerance and open-mindedness of the era helped create the conditions that made peace and prosperity possible. Stated another way, cultural and religious tolerance isn't a product of prosperous times; rather it is an essential cause. Such tolerance can be developed in an individual regardless of his or her social and economic position. Conversely, peace and prosperity don't spontaneously arise on their own; certain conditions must be in place before they can take root, grow, flower. Tyranny and intolerance are not those conditions. Again, I'm writing in general terms. Central Asia, like the rest of the world at that time, was often embroiled in war, and many of its leaders were models of tyranny. But, looked at broadly today, we can see that Central Asia also set a standard for the peaceful coexistence of different cultures and religions that our "enlightened" Western world has since too often failed to match.

And most economists will tell you that ensuring free and open markets is the best recipe for economic success. The vast open market that was the Silk Road was more than a marketplace of goods—it was just as important for the exchange of ideas it facilitated. This has been its lasting legacy.

The implications of this are numerous, perhaps the most obvious being that Central Asia should open up to other faiths, even welcome them. Why, then, in direct contrast to its past, is the region so closed off today? When Kazakhstan expelled a group of talented doctors because they were also missionaries, it may have been good in preserving the "traditional" culture, but in a country with a lack of qualified medical professionals, it was arguably not the best development choice.

In my time there, if a Central Asian was taught English by a foreigner, it was most likely by either a U.S. Peace Corps volunteer or a missionary. Representatives of both groups have a message, and both promote "foreign" ideas. What exactly is the difference between the two?

Preaching to all creation

As a Peace Corps volunteer, I was an officially sworn-in representative of the U.S. government, forbidden to proselytize on two subjects—religion and politics—or to work directly with anyone involved in such activities. I believe this was wise; as a guest in Kazakhstan, I was invited to work within their cultural and political framework and offer suggestions for its improvement, not to criticize or overhaul it based on my own personal philosophies.

Because of this, and more so because of my childhood questioning of the Christian Church, I had negative feelings towards missionaries, even before I encountered them in Kazakhstan. But once I did, I was pleasantly surprised to find them intellectually open and friendly, some even downright engaging.

Being highly visible in my community through the many seminars I presented and English clubs I conducted, I naturally came into contact with a wide variety of people with a wide variety of beliefs, both locals and foreigners. Befriending Christians certainly wasn't forbidden any more than being one, as long as I didn't become involved in any proselytizing activities. During my stay, I knew a number of missionaries from all over the world: America, Switzerland, the British Isles. When one missionary couple who had lived in Kazakhstan for five years left to return to England, I asked them what their plans were.

"We don't know," the husband said, smiling. "We simply trust that God will lead us to the next step." His calm demeanor demonstrated to me that his was no foolish blind faith but rather something genuine that he had tapped into, something deeper than I can explain. I must confess, I felt a little jealous, given my own uncertain situation at the time in finishing up my commitment to Peace Corps and not knowing what my next step would be. I certainly didn't feel calm.

Interestingly, neither this couple nor any of the other missionaries I have known seem comfortable with the word "missionary."

Another missionary, Susan, a lively, articulate woman who spent more than a decade living in foreign countries as a Christian missionary, accepts her title especially reluctantly: "Hmmm … 'missionary' … I hate that word because of all the baggage attached to it, but there seems to be no escaping from it. If I lived in my home country, I would be called a pastor or a minister or a church worker, but because I've been involved with expressions of Christianity all over the world, that makes me a missionary."

Another thoughtful individual, Greg, wrote to me, "Seeing as I avoid the often misunderstood term of missionary, Kazakhstan citizens usually treat me as an English teacher, another form of 'missions' I suppose, or is that 'cultural imperialism'?"

⋇

So what does it mean to be a missionary? The second of two senses defined in *The American Heritage Dictionary* is, "One who attempts to convert others to a particular doctrine or set of principles." I like this definition, for it properly, I believe, leaves out mention of religion and focuses instead on the broader framework in which religion rests, that is, its doctrines and principles.

Equally as significant is the first sense defined, "A propagandist for a belief or cause." Propaganda today carries a deeply negative connotation, one conjuring images of Stalin's purges and other unchecked Orwellian nightmares. It often is used for dark, manipulative purposes and, as Orwell knew, is centrally featured in totalitarian regimes. Yet it wasn't always regarded this way. It was initially used by the Catholic Church in the name of an organization established to further missionary activity. It didn't begin taking on more questionable connotations until the nineteenth century. The word itself comes from the Latin verb propagare, which means "to propagate"—that is, propaganda is simply a way to "grow" or "broadcast" an idea, broadcast here also meaning the way a farmer traditionally sowed a field. Taken in this sense, anyone who has ever tried to persuade another of anything—which is everyone—has been a propagandist.

In my critical thinking classes, I explained that there are two kinds of propagandists, or "peddlers," a term I use to emphasize the notion of selling ideas: political or ideological peddlers, those who attempt to persuade in order to gain something personally—such as money, power, or influence—and philosophical peddlers, those who attempt to persuade because they are motivated purely by philosophy (the "love of wisdom"). In theory, this is a good distinction. In practice, I'm not sure it's true, for even the most magnanimous humanist and spiritual masters, in disseminating their wisdom freely, gain tangible benefits, if only in knowing their words are helping others. The master who teaches without expectation of any profit, as naturally as a seed falls from a tree, is one in a million. The rest of us are, to varying degrees, political peddlers.

All missionaries, by virtue of being human, do not work for purely altruistic reasons but rather expect something in return. They may expect to see quantifiable results—numbers of people "saved." They may, either consciously or unconsciously, seek stores of treasure in heaven for their efforts on earth. At the very least, like loving gardeners tending their flower beds, they expect the ideas that they have planted to grow and to blossom.

⁂

People of faith should have the freedom to speak their beliefs. To witness is an especially important aspect of Christian life. "Go into the world and preach the good news to all creation," Jesus is quoted in Mark 16:15. But where is the line between preaching the good news and forcing it on someone? Pressure can be subtle, as I learned from my own experience.

My disenchantment with my non-denominational Congregational church coincided with the time it began growing overly emotional in a way that to me seemed insincere. This involved a shift away from open discourse and toward displays such as waving hands, shouting praises, groaning with the Spirit (capital "S"), and similar theatrics, especially during prayer times. Everyone's eyes were supposed to be closed then, but I kept mine open and observed the congregation. What to blind ears sounded spontaneous and joyful to watchful eyes appeared calculated and timid. Many members of the congregation actually looked around the sanctuary first before "spontaneously" being overcome by the Spirit, and I noticed that these displays fed on each other, always starting slowly and growing more numerous as people became more comfortable with what was going on. This was the beginning of my doubts about the church.

The pressure the members of that congregation felt was largely self-made. The pastor didn't openly dictate that his parishioners make those displays; their own need for approval and inclusion within the group dictated it. But I wonder how much the pastor understood this. To say that he was completely unaware of it is to assign to this educated and specially trained man a shocking lack of knowledge about basic human psychology. To say that he was fully aware is to assign to him a conscious desire to manipulate, for tacitly encouraging such displays is manipulation. The truth is most likely that his understanding of his role and the degree to which he used it to manipulate people probably fell somewhere between these two extremes.

But why this pressure at all? Shouldn't something supposedly so good sell itself?

Sometimes there's a blurry line between giving and selling. What is offered at no financial cost can often have subtle or hidden emotional ones.

So, to come back to what it means to be a missionary: my working definition is anyone who has an idea they want to grow with the expectation of something in exchange, either for the idea or the effort in growing it, for we're all human, and we cannot, unless we have undergone the most rigorous mental discipline, avoid this. Lastly, it also involves intent: if you are a teacher, but the main reason you came to Central Asia—to anywhere—is to spread the Christian gospel, then your teaching work cannot hide that you are a missionary.

Still, missionaries continue to hide this, which raises some interesting and difficult moral issues.

Moral implications

Missionary work, while foreign to Kazakhstan's and Turkic cultures generally, is freely permitted by law. The only requirement [of] the missionaries is to respect the laws of the country and to conduct their activity in a transparent and reasonable manner respectful to our citizenry.

—"Freedom of Religion and Interethnic Accord," Embassy of Kazakhstan to the United States and Canada

When I was living in a village my first summer in Kazakhstan, I would sometimes watch TV with my host family. The World Cup soccer tournament was being played then, and while the Kazakhstani national team hadn't qualified, my host brother Adik took a special interest in this—the first World Cup hosted in Asia. My familiarity with the sport made it easier for me to follow the announcers with my beginner's Russian. There was also one English-language news program that ran on Sundays at 10:00 p.m. On a particular feature on Kazakhstani journalistic ethics, one guest stated that propaganda was good it if was in the cause of promoting a better life. Other subjects, he said, should be covered more independently, in a more unbiased way.

It's true that not all propaganda is the same. Is our propaganda—the ideas we want to grow—meant to enlighten or to manipulate? It's easy to tell the difference. Enlightened ideas will help others develop and grow their own senses of discernment, common sense, and critical thinking, and these lead to the empowerment of individuals. Manipulation leads to disempowerment. The fruits of each will clearly show which seeds were planted.

Of course, manipulators try their best to ensure that those being manipulated don't know it, or feel confused enough not to resist it, or even come to distrust their own thoughts and experiences entirely. Such has been played for centuries, and it's still routinely played today by anyone from abusive partners to egomaniacal political leaders.

Propaganda can be either positive or negative. It can include honest methods of persuasion such as sound logical arguments and sincere emotional entreaties as well as those forms of rhetoric that are intended to be deceitful, such as gaslighting, fearmongering, spin, and outright lying.

⨳

In addition to the missionaries already mentioned, I met and peripherally knew a few of approximately twenty recent American university graduates sent to Kazakhstan as teachers. Generally, the work of this group, from reports of my own students who interacted with them, was good. Diana, whom I ran into often at various locations around Shymkent, was especially pleasant, always greeting me with a warm smile.

However, Diana and her colleagues also were, from my very first meeting with them, less than candid about their true intentions. I was eating at an Uzbek restaurant with a group of friends, enjoying a typical meal of rice, grilled mutton kebabs, lepyoshka bread, and tea, when the newcomers stopped by. We asked them the usual questions: How long have you been here? How do you like it? Do you speak any Russian or Kazakh? To our surprise, they'd had no language training and very little formal training at all, so we asked what group sponsored them. Here they became extremely vague, and I had the distinct feeling that they were being deliberately evasive. I continued to press the point, respectfully but somewhat determinedly, but was unable to find out any more than they were teachers and their sponsor was a non-denominational group, representing various beliefs.

With this last piece of information, I suspected that they were missionaries, but I wasn't certain until one of my students, Zhanat, complained about a meeting she attended. This was ostensibly an "English club" led by Diana's group, and it included the games, discussions, and refreshments typical of such clubs. After these were over, the leaders asked those in attendance to sit and listen to a series of speeches by local people. At first, it was unclear what was going on, but slowly Zhanat and two of her friends understood that these were former Muslims who had converted to Christianity. Zhanat and her friends—like most of those in the room, in the city—were Muslim, and they grew increasingly angry as they listened. Finally, in the middle of one person's "witnessing," they stood up and walked out. Zhanat later told me she had felt deceived that this group would advertise hosting an English club meeting when it was essentially an evangelizing assembly.

Other problems arose. Radio ads began airing, offering free English lessons with Peace Corps volunteers—except the Peace Corps knew nothing about these ads. My students and other local friends told me of meeting "Peace Corps volunteers," but when I asked who, the names and descriptions of these people matched no one I knew. There were only six of us in our oblast (administrative region) at the time, so obviously some group was spreading disinformation in order to justify or perhaps cover its own activities. Alarmed by this, the Peace Corps sent two of its local staff members to investigate, and they eventually discovered that the radio ads had been paid for by missionaries. I took it personally because it had the potential to color my work.

One week, I was unable to attend my regular English club, but a fellow volunteer did, and he reported that Diana and another young woman also attended. By this time, even local people who hadn't had direct contact with these Americans were beginning to suspect they were missionaries. At one point during the club, Anatoly, a jolly but also very direct ethnic Russian, turned to the young women and asked, "Are you missionaries?" Without hesitation, Diana did what on the surface would seem to be a very un-Christian thing to do.

She lied.

"No," she stated bluntly.

⨳

How does one distinguish between the broadcasting of constructive new ideas and the subversive undermining of existing traditions? And how should a sensitive human react to the latter? For all cultures, in order to remain vital, must have their traditions challenged, else they risk becoming isolated or irrelevant.

I didn't know how to feel when I heard the story of Diana at my English club. On the one hand, I was upset, for she and her organization were not conducting themselves "in a transparent and reasonable manner." On the other hand, this was understandable. Many missionaries have been kicked out of their respective Central Asian countries, or worse, once their true intentions have been discovered.

In Turkmenistan, dozens of missionaries have been deported. In particular, Turkmen officials openly declared that they would "strangle" local Baptist churches. Even in more liberal Kazakhstan and Kyrgyzstan, political and social pressure often drives religious groups underground. Occasionally, this can result in violence. While I was living in Kazakhstan in 2004, Presbyterian missionaries were twice attacked and robbed in the village of Zhaksy. In a perverse twist, the attackers forced the missionaries, blindfolded, into a truck and attempted to coerce them into accepting Islam.

Such outright and inexcusable persecution is rare. But all five post-Soviet Central Asian countries have laws requiring religious groups to register with the government, and these laws are sometimes used to harass or deport missionaries, even when their activities are otherwise lawful and peaceful.

These governmental attitudes are poor reflections of the centuries-old tradition of enlightened Islamic scholarship and culture and the millennia-old tradition of religious tolerance indigenous to the Silk Road. Authorities justify it with the rationale that missionaries come on false pretenses and use deceitful methods to attract members.

A struggle over process

Is it moral for missionaries to come to Central Asia on false pretenses? Is it justifiable to provide false pretenses for anything? The answer is, most would agree, a pragmatic yes, at least sometimes. For example, had Stalin-era Soviet Muslims and Christians admitted to the authorities that they met clandestinely, they would have been imprisoned, possibly killed, and their mosques and churches appropriated or destroyed (those that were left after Sovietization, that is). In Central Asia, these two faiths held many people together in the face of extreme hardship and allowed the line of cultural transmission to remain open. These benefits easily justified secrecy.

Today, missionaries also do good work, teaching, providing food and shelter to the poor, and offering essential health services. But do their good works justify what is essentially a lie? This is an especially intriguing question given that many fundamentalist Christian sects would argue that good works alone do *not* justify anything—only believing in Jesus will bring salvation. This stands in contrast to the Sufi idea that self-development is essential in growing closer to God. Following only the letter of the law isn't enough; good works also count. Or, as a verse from Imam Malik ibn Anas (b. 711) recounts,

> Whoever has the outer Law without the inner Reality has left the right way;
> Whoever has the inner Reality without the outer Law is a heretic;
> Whoever joins the two of them has realization.

Both Islam and Christianity acknowledge God; in fact, Islam recognizes this as the same God, for like Christianity and Judaism, it traces its roots through the same line of prophets all the way back to Abraham. In other words, this isn't a struggle over God. It's a struggle over *process*—who has the best path.

Admittedly, the differences aren't small. Christians see Jesus as God incarnate, one-third of the Holy Trinity; Muslims see Jesus as a prophet, albeit an important one, in a long line that finally ends with the Prophet Muhammad.

Interestingly, while in my personal talks with Muslims in Central Asia they have consistently opposed Christian missionaries, at the same time they have consistently expressed the belief that the Muslim

God and Christian God are the same. Despite the obvious differences between Judaism, Christianity, and Islam, the Qur'an actually offers many teachings on their essential unity, including these from 'Abdullah Yusuf 'Ali's free-verse translation, *The Meaning of the Holy Qur'an*, cited first by the surah (chapter) and then the ayah (verse): "It is He Who sent down / To thee (step by step), / In truth, the Book, / Confirming what went before it; / And He sent down the Law / (Of Moses) and the Gospel (of Jesus)" (3:3); "And dispute ye not / With the People of the Book [Jews and Christians] … / But say, 'We believe / In the Revelation which has / Come down to us and in that / Which came down to you; / Our God and your God / Is One. …'" (29:46).

To some Christians, this is perhaps not so clear. But such doctrinal differences shouldn't detract from both religions' shared spiritual goal—reunion with the Source of everything, to "burn one's self before the One." If you're a Muslim, Christian, or Jew, live your path fully, but why try to force others into the footprint your foot is in?

Everyone has the right to decide their own views. No one should decide for another, particularly through coercion. While to believe one's personal views are right for one's self is perfectly fine, even natural, to believe one's personal views are right for everyone is narrow-minded, and any attempt to enforce those views on others, however benignly it might be presented, is a form of violence. Some missionaries are reviled because they take the latter approach, or are perceived to do so. But the definition of *missionary* doesn't include this. It is only "bad" ones who do it.

A good teacher—or a good parent, or a good friend—presents information that allows others to make the strongest, most informed decisions for themselves. Our job is to discover what truth means to us individually and, if we wish, speak it openly without pushing our versions of truth on those around us. Others may accept our words or not—may build on them, adapt them, or ignore them altogether, as they see fit. The world is plenty large enough to accommodate this. I do not in any way buy into the idea that we now live in what has been called a "post-truth" world. The speed at which information travels today makes it seem like there are more irreconcilable ideas than ever before, but the reality is that humans have always argued the validity of one viewpoint or another and will continue to do so. Our choice is to engage with each other peacefully or not.

The religious struggle over process isn't just being waged in Central Asia but all around the world—sectarian fighting is almost as likely to feature Christians versus Christians as it is Hindus versus Muslims or Muslims versus Jews. "The most drastic example I can think of is Rwanda," my missionary friend Susan declared of the fighting that, in 1994, killed eight hundred thousand people in one hundred days. "On the Sunday before the genocide started, something like 80 percent of the population, from both tribes, was in church, calling themselves Christians. And these were enthusiastic churches, with loud, lively, passionate singing, and lots of passionate preaching. But the problem was that many of those people had signed up for a cheap gospel that said accept Jesus in your heart and you'll go to heaven. They hadn't been challenged that becoming a Christian means Jesus will ask you to lay down old hatreds and prejudices. They hadn't been told that there was no longer any choice about loving your neighbor."

It really comes down to the question of what makes people want to change others. With respect to Christians, I don't believe it can be explained by simply stating that they want to bring the good news to the world as directed by the Bible. If that were the case, then why did one conservative Protestant I know call Catholicism "a cult"—a contemporary echo of old Protestant-Catholic tensions that have caused countless wars and millions of deaths over the centuries all over the world?

A policy of plunder

"Why do Americans hate Muslims?"

Several of my friends and I were asked this on numerous occasions in Central Asia, particularly right after the United States invaded Iraq.

It is not an idle question on the part of the local people. For many, a very real and great fear motivates their asking. As part of his work, one friend (later a colleague) of mine was attempting to recruit applicants for a special program to send Islamic leaders to the United States for several weeks. He had a tremendously difficult time doing so because of the potential applicants' deep distrust of the U.S. government.

"Will you put us in a concentration camp?" they asked seriously. "Will we be allowed to come back to Kazakhstan? Why do Americans hate Muslims so much?"

That was in 2003 in another part of the world. Today, Muslims in our own country, many of them U.S. citizens, are asking essentially the same questions.

While America's war in Iraq was supported by the governments of all five post-Soviet Central Asian nations, their citizens were overwhelmingly against it. It's not the place of this essay to examine the reasons for the invasion. But having lived over there, I can report that it had a disastrous effect on our image with the Islamic world. It did not help win the "hearts and minds" of the people. Nor have the words of many American religious and political leaders, who often seem to deliberately widen the rift between Muslims and Christians rather than attempt to close it.

In the lead-up to the war, Pat Robertson declared it wasn't just a religious struggle but "a clash of cultures," as if each religion was practiced by a single culture within homogenous borders. Fellow evangelist Jerry Falwell one-upped him by calling the Prophet Muhammad "a terrorist." The religious bigotry has only grown in intensity since then, culminating in a proposed ban on all Muslims entering the U.S.

Admittedly, these men and others like them do not represent the majority of Americans, or even all Christians. But they do wield tremendous influence and so carry an equally tremendous responsibility. Those in their position should show greater sensitivity and more awareness of the wider world around them. Eight people were killed and some fifty injured in India in rioting during a protest of Falwell's statement. Whether intended or not, the effects of such untempered speech are clear: it has helped normalize inflammatory rhetoric in public quarters and lowered the level of civil discourse in our country.

Such insensitivity is not new, however, nor is it limited to America. The Russian government in Tsarist times often struck a similar attitude toward its Muslim subjects, whom it viewed as fodder to feed its growing empire. One October 1864 memo from the Ministry of Foreign Affairs to the Tsar, written in the midst of a push to capture several cities ever deeper on Central Asian soil—Turkistan, Shymkent, Tashkent, Samarkand—admitted that the Russian empire, "influenced by the insistent demands of our trade, and some mysterious but irresistible urge towards the east, was steadily moving into the heart of the Steppe"—very poetic language for naked imperialism.

This same mysterious but irresistible urge seems to have beckoned the Bolsheviks who followed. At a 1921 party congress, they declared that "if the strengthening of the center requires it, a policy of plunder in the borderlands [i.e., Central Asia] would be proper and correct."

Once their Muslim citizens were subjugated and plundered, the Soviets stepped up their efforts, attempting not just to expel Islam from their new socialist experiment but religion in all its sundry manifestations, what they called "medieval hangovers." People were targeted for recruitment as allahsizlar, or "godless people," to assist the Movement of the Godless in Sovietizing the local cultures that had been absorbed into the new empire. Despite being deemed semiautonomous, rule was only nominally local; the central authority was in Moscow. The native peoples were largely "otherized," looked at as exotic foreigners more than equal citizens. In theory, the Soviets wanted to rectify these injustices and bring equality to the region, but in many ways they ended up marginalizing native peoples even more.

Communism, while materialistic, actually turned Marxist values into a religion, with all its attendant dogma and blind faith. Its "missionary work" was ruthlessly unsubtle and efficient. In his chapter from the essay collection *Civil Society in Central Asia*, Reuel Hanks, an American professor who taught as a Fulbright Scholar in Uzbekistan, relates that he heard stories "from students and colleagues of parents and/or grandparents being forced to drink or eat during Ramadan, of pressures to publicly consume alcohol during Communist Party or Komsomol functions. ..." Of the more than twenty-six thousand mosques in the Russian empire in its last years, only a few hundred survived into the 1980s.

From the ancient Silk Road, that massive, interconnected network of missionary routes, to what has been called the New Silk Road, the massive oil and gas pipelines that connect the region to the rest of the world, foreigners have always looked to Central Asia for something: grazing land, access to trade routes, a strategic location, natural resources—or souls to be saved.

Given this larger cultural context, it is little wonder why many Muslims there feel threatened by Christian missionaries. For however peaceful their intentions may seem, the suspicion always lurks that there's still a battle going on, not over turf but over "hearts and minds"—over differing ways of life.

Business, bombs, books, or beans

Although being a religious missionary can be risky in Central Asia, they still come by the hundreds. In Kazakhstan, Christian proselytizing is possibly the number two profession of Americans in the country, behind only oil—"evangelicals and oilmen," as I once overheard someone at the U.S. embassy in Almaty remark. In Kyrgyzstan, gold and other mineral resources are the lure, gas in Turkmenistan; in all five countries, it's airbases or schools or the opportunity to offer humanitarian aid—

"business, bombs, books, or beans," as my friend Greg put it. "They each have a purpose that can be described as missionary."

As mentioned earlier, I believe all missionaries have a message, engage in persuasion, and expect to gain something for their efforts. Under that definition, who is not a missionary?

My answer is that everyone is a missionary. This includes the governments of the Central Asian republics as well as the foreigners, secular and scientific enterprises right along with the more overtly religious ones. "Even proponents of the Linux operating system use terms like 'evangelism,' 'advocacy,' and 'conversion' in relation to spreading their ideas," notes Greg. So do American business people, to whom "free-market enterprise" is the gospel and *The Wall Street Journal* the Bible.

Certainly, every teacher is a missionary. There is no way to present objectively the sum of all knowledge in any field in any classroom, and deciding which pieces to throw out and which to pass along inevitably relies on personal biases. In short, teachers teach what they think is right and thus propagate their own beliefs in their students, who then knowingly or unknowingly spread them.

The Soviets understood this function of education well; many fundamentalist schools and universities today do, too, both Christian and Islamic.

※

We're all on a mission—we all have an objective or purpose in life. For some, it's to raise a family. For others, it's to help their companies grow. Many want to share the values of social and environmental justice. In the U.S., the Smokey the Bear campaign to help prevent wildfires along with anti-littering, anti-smoking, and other public health messages are all examples of propaganda used for positive ends. Even in the Soviet Union, stunningly designed propaganda posters could include messages about such topics as the importance of exercising, maintaining good personal hygiene, recognizing women's rights, and drinking less alcohol. It's important to acknowledge that these are legitimate.

Today, people are comfortable with spreading their views widely, even to total strangers. The internet has been democratizing, at least in the sense of allowing a broad range of voices. But it has come at certain costs, the lack of decorum and spread of false ideas most prominent among them.

Given this, we have a special responsibility to be respectful of our fellow humans. Discussion—civil, engaged, equally mutual discussion—is more important than ever. Such discussion requires each participant to bring their views to the table. These views may seem so opposed to each other that they may be completely misunderstood by the respective participants, but understanding isn't a condition necessary for communication to be successful. All that's needed is openness. Communication is a process, and if it is engaged in sincerely by all sides with complete openness, then understanding is one possible result.

Those with the gentlest hearts and most generous gifts to offer are often too shy or afraid to speak out and spread their message. It's time to engage, for good people of all faiths and cultures to come together and act as a powerful curative to the gaslighters, fearmongers, spin masters, and outright liars. For every seed of division sown, one must be propagated of unity. For every message of fear and enmity, one must be propagated of love.

⁙

What did I expect in return for coming to Central Asia? What do I expect for writing this?

My idealism was a major reason I joined the Peace Corps. What may seem naïvely optimistic ideals to some, I truly believe in—ideals of the basic spiritual unity of humankind despite outward religious, social, and political differences. But to leave it at that is to tell only half the story. I was also well aware of my desire for adventure and challenge, which living within a foreign culture and my related travels certainly provided. As a writer, I knew this stimulation would be good for my creativity. It was and still is.

As a native speaker with previous teaching experience, I may have given my talents freely, but despite my title "volunteer," I didn't give them for free; most Peace Corps volunteers will tell you that they received at least as much in return, and I was no exception. The experiences I had, the friendships I made, the growth I experienced in my two years are unforgettable, and I can't imagine my life without them.

As a teacher there, I was a missionary, an educational missionary. When I taught Emerson and Thoreau in my advanced American literature class, I taught about more than the stout American individualism they espoused—I exposed the transcendentalist ideas that lay behind this, the German and Indian philosophy which informed it all (both authors were ardent students of the *Bhagavad-Gita*, the cornerstone of Hindu spiritualism).

After completing my Peace Corps service, I managed the Kazakhstan and Kyrgyzstan region of a program that sends Eurasian professionals to study at the graduate level in America. I believe supporting such programs, including the Peace Corps, is one of the best ways that the United States spends its foreign aid dollars, and I want this idea to grow; I'm a propagandist, an educational missionary still.

As to what I expected in writing this … I wanted to write about history and human possibility, to explore a difficult and controversial issue and offer some alternative ways to think about it, to help others form informed positions on it, whatever those positions may be. I especially wanted to present information that many Americans—in particular, many Christian Americans—don't encounter through the mainstream media.

In the end, I am offering my view of the world and exposing myself for who I am—a true believer in the inherent potential of all humans to find their way to God, on their own terms, in their own time.

Perhaps this is even a plea, a plea for religious pluralism. Or maybe a prayer in essay form. As the Quranic translator Yusuf 'Ali wrote in the preface to his 1934 first edition, "It is good to make this personal confession, to an age in which it is in the highest degree unfashionable to speak of religion or spiritual peace or consolation, an age in which words like these draw forth only derision, pity, or contempt."

Traveling and the universality of religions

When I was sixteen, due to my church's overemphasis on emotion and inability to engage my intellect and intuition, I left. More than three decades later, after a long, broad study of other religions and philosophies, I've come to recognize and embrace many of the universal truths represented in Christianity, a recognition and embrace that have come on my own terms, in comparison to the universal truths in other religions.

My search has led me to explore other cultures not only in books but directly, physically. In my travels throughout the British Isles and Ireland, I visited some of the famous and inspiring places of the Christian world: Westminster Abbey in London and Gloucester Cathedral in Gloucester, St. Patrick's Cathedral and Christ's Church Cathedral in Dublin. Later, I visited some of the famous and inspiring places of the Muslim world: the Sultan Ahmet Camii (better known as the "Blue Mosque") and Süleymaniye Camii in Istanbul, the Jama Masjid ("Great Mosque") in Delhi, the Registan complex in Samarkand. Whether surrounded by the magnificent complexity of Christian architecture—the ornate columns, carved figures, and stained-glass windows—or the exquisite simplicity of Islamic architecture—the clean lines, airy spaces, and seamlessly integrated ornamental details—I felt a tangible sense of peace at each no matter the religion or sect represented.

Throughout history, the holy places of one culture have always been built atop the ruins of another culture's. Symbolically, this is supposed to show the power of the new religion over the old. But this symbolism means nothing if the old religion isn't recognized as being a threat to the new one. It saddens me to think that the search for truth is so often seen as a competition where only one team can win rather than a party to which we're all invited.

The more I travel, the smaller the world becomes but the larger my wonder of it grows. I'm reminded of a saying of Muhammad bin Ali Ibn Arabi (b. 1165): "Whoever engages in travel will arrive!" Though it's a metaphor for one embarking on a spiritual journey, ultimately, all of life is a spiritual journey.

Of course, one doesn't need physically to travel halfway around the world to find his or her spiritual truth. Every major religion, in some form or another—when its holy words are distilled to their very purest form—teaches that outer reality is simply a manifestation of inner reality, and that outer reality is ultimately all illusion anyway. The real way to get somewhere is to travel through one's own soul.

A friend of mine in the Peace Corps experienced problems similar to those I faced upon first arriving in the region, though hers held far deeper implications. Despite having taught successfully for more than a year at her university in Turkistan, being respected both by her peers and her students for leading a variety of academic activities outside the classroom, including a highly popular English club, the university's president accused her of being a missionary and expelled her from the campus. He later recanted and apologized, but it was too late; she ended up teaching 280 kilometers to the northwest in Kyzylorda. The incident was a stark reminder that the deep suspicion of anything foreign, and particularly of missionaries, real or imagined, remained as strong as ever.

Central Asia once showed the world how open discourse can promote human flourishing, eudaimonia. Sufi missionaries helped shape the character of the region in a positive way.

Central Asia has also shown how tyranny and closed discourse can lead to stagnation and suffering.

We must find a way to share with each other the good news of what we feel passionate about while at the same time respecting that we won't always agree. Are missionaries genuinely exposing local populations to broader ideas than they otherwise have access to, and are the locals then allowed to choose freely from among these ideas—the old and the new? If so, then these missionaries are truly doing nothing more than any good teacher would—revealing the wonder of the world by offering options and helping their "students" develop the intellectual tools to make good choices.

But if missionaries present their ideas in the context not of offering a choice but of presenting "the truth," then they are doing what bad teachers and dictators do—demanding blind obeisance to the party line. It can be a belief in transcendentalism or communist materialism; it doesn't matter.

Christianity—at least its fundamentalist sects—could benefit from the Sufi idea that personal growth and good works *do* count. The idea that all we need is to accept Jesus in our hearts may save souls but does little to help those still stuck on earth. And Islam—at least in Central Asia—could benefit from more interaction with other faiths, just as it once did during its Golden Age. There needs to be a give and take, an opening, on both sides. As it is, both are too closed.

Living in another culture has helped me understand my own culture better. Studying other religions has helped me understand my religion, the religion of my childhood, better. The process isn't, and shouldn't be, threatening.

It has led me to believe there is no such religion as "mine" or "yours" or "theirs." In today's Information Age, I have access to the wisdom of all the faiths of recorded history. The internet doesn't recognize the clannishness that kept one faith tied to one geographic region; the ideas themselves no longer recognize this skin color or that last name or those modes of dress. In this sense, we may have finally arrived at a time when "all will hear the word of God."

In the end, no one really has his or her own religious heritage—Islam for Central Asians, Christianity for Euro-Americans, Buddhism for East Asians. All we have is the religious heritage of the world and what we as individuals make of it. The path isn't as important as the sincerity of the seeker.

MORE THAN TENGE AND TIYN

Kairat, dark-haired and bespectacled, possessed a curious combination of reticence and confidence, sometimes saying little and sometimes almost jumping out of his chair with excitement when he had an answer to a question. Julia, pale and blonde, exuded a calm steadiness, with clear diction and little trace of an accent. Elena showed her seriousness with an unwavering gaze under arched eyebrows, though her eyes flashed whenever her ironic sense of humor was engaged. Anton was the trickster of the group, with a wide crooked grin, his hair usually disheveled, as proficient in computer science as he was in English; I always suspected he was the talented genius who had programmed the computers in the university's library to automatically insert "Oy, blin!"—a mild expletive in Russian that roughly translates as, "Oh, poop!"—every time a comma was typed.

These were some of my students when I was a Peace Corps English instructor in Kazakhstan. Teaching them was fun, and I had high expectations for both them and myself. Early in my service, however, I had also seen the need for balancing my enthusiasm as an idealistic volunteer against the realities I faced: a demanding and constantly changing schedule, decayed infrastructure, and an utter lack of adequate books for my classes. I learned to be content with the small victories.

I considered the response to my resume and interviewing class one such victory. The information was entirely new to my students, who felt it might give them an edge with Western organizations or relatively progressive Kazakhstani companies. Tired of living in a transition economy barely a decade removed from the collapse of the Soviet Union and the birth of an entirely new country, young people eagerly sought anything that might lead to better jobs and salaries. I was glad to help in this small but tangible way. Still, I couldn't help wondering, how many of them would actually be able to use the most important skills I could teach them—how to be intellectually curious and independent, to maximize their creative potential, and to think outside of the box? Was it possible for me to help them discover their true passions in life, let alone develop these?

During my last semester, I learned that my students had applied for only one educational grant between them.

"Why should we apply?" Julia coolly replied when I asked her class about it.

"Everyone knows you have to pay a bribe to win," Elena quickly added, which the others loudly affirmed.

More than any other aspect of life there, I had the most difficult time adjusting to this. The Western world has always had its own particular, deep-seated issues with corruption. Yet I had never encountered it as systemically as I did in Central Asia, especially in everyday business.

Not everyone engaged in it, of course, and certainly no one admitted to liking the practice; most spoke out passionately against it. It was seen as something out of their control, unavoidable if they wanted to get anything done or get anywhere in life. Good jobs often went to relatives or unqualified applicants who paid for them—people were not hired for work based on merit but rather on whether they could afford the bribe. Kickbacks trickled upward, so the higher in authority one rose, the more illicit money one could receive, which is why the higher positions cost the most. Bribery was common not just with government officials and police officers but also with safety and health inspectors, utility meter readers, and teachers. Traffic offenses and criminal judgments could be avoided or overturned with bribes to the police or judiciary. Inspections such as those regarding food safety or building codes could be avoided for a bribe. While I never saw or even heard of it at my university, it was widely accepted that many teachers at all levels of education accepted bribes in exchange for more favorable grades.

I gave a dozen workshops on education to Central Asian teachers at conferences throughout Kazakhstan, and I usually brought up corruption as being an issue to tackle, though never at length. Once I mentioned it in passing during the course of a presentation. Afterward, the rector of the university where the conference was being held spent several minutes responding animatedly on how corruption did not exist in Kazakhstan's institutions.

This annoyed me even as I understood it. Corruption may have been widespread, but it was still illegal. The rector had to cover his educational assets. More than that, it was hard to blame the poor teachers, whose salaries were so meager they didn't even cover rent, let alone other bills, and were often paid months behind schedule. Some teachers outright sold higher grades to the more affluent students. More conscientious teachers provided extra tutoring outside of the classroom for a fee, which supplemented their salaries while also helping their students. All the teachers I knew worked from early in the morning to long into the evening, and as most were female—Central Asian society in the early twenty-first century remained very much male dominated—they still faced an entire day's worth of cooking, cleaning, and taking care of the children when they returned home.

It was a world where money mattered immensely, though not in the same way as in the States, where our aspirations are, by and large, for increasing levels of luxury. In Kazakhstan, especially in those hardscrabble days, it was a matter of survival.

My students felt helpless to change this. And I felt helpless to do more than provide some basic English skills that would give them, perhaps, a foot up in the business world, even as I always hoped that somehow I could also introduce them to more, something deeper and intangible, something that couldn't be equated in dollars and cents—or in this case, tenge and tiyn.

So, while their feelings about the equity of the educational grant application process were understandable, I still passionately challenged them to apply to every grant and fellowship program they were qualified for, especially the American and European ones, which I assured were judged independently and run fairly. I knew from my own continuing experience just how mind-expanding living in a foreign country could be.

Kairat remained glum. He had applied for a particular U.S. fellowship two years in a row and actually made it to the semi-finalist round the second year. Yet rather than see this as progress, he saw his ultimate non-selection as a sign of his failings. I urged him to see the positives in his experience, to learn from them, and to try again, always to try again. He said that due to the age limitation, the coming year was the last he could apply, but he would think about it.

My two years in Peace Corps went by, as they do for so many, too quickly. I felt sad to leave one of the best teaching experiences of my life, a feeling intensified by the many well-wishes and heartfelt requests to remain at my university that I received. The stubborn idealist in me still wondered if in the greater scheme of life I had really made a significant difference.

※

I spent little time transitioning into the regular workforce again, remaining in Central Asia to become manager of a prestigious fellowship program in Kazakhstan and Kyrgyzstan. Within three months I went from making a couple hundred dollars a month to a couple thousand and more, from living in a one-room apartment with a fold-out couch to a suite with a separate bedroom and a real bed. Suddenly I could afford to take taxis instead of waiting for the packed buses or marshrutki (shared vans or mini-buses), to shop at the brand-new supermarkets in addition to the local bazaars, to eat at some very nice restaurants. Gone were the days of cold, under-equipped classrooms and late English language clubs after a long day. Now it was business lunches and social events at the American ambassador's home.

Despite all this, I strangely didn't feel as satisfied. I was now helping administer some of the very fellowships I had encouraged my students to consider, an essential part of the whole equation. These fellowships offered important opportunities to those highly qualified students who earned them—opportunities they and their families otherwise never could afford. Those students in turn went on to enrich the American institutions where they studied, broadening the worldviews of American students by introducing them to peers from a part of the world to which they otherwise would never be exposed. To this day, I believe such cultural exchanges are staggeringly more valuable than the small cost of offering them. What was missing?

I found that I missed living so much closer to the people, as I did as a volunteer. When I had taught, I was fully part of my community, not just another ex-pat working overseas. In my new job, I still worked with local people, but no longer as an equal; I was now one of the bosses. I still had an obligation to my job, though not necessarily to my community. I tried hard to treat it the same, but the dynamic was completely different.

While many of the then-current volunteers in Kazakhstan envied my position, I found myself envying theirs. I missed the face-to-face opportunities teaching provided, to be an everyday role model, to directly help guide young lives. My counterpart—the person who was the point of contact between the Peace Corps and my host institution—

had actively solicited to have a volunteer placed at her university, and she made sure to support me and utilize me well. I was busy, which was good, but even better, I felt needed. As a fellowship manager, I repeatedly heard of how our applicants, all working professionals, had been positively influenced in some way by Peace Corps volunteers.

This returned to me full circle when I learned that my former student Kairat, on his third and final try, had been selected as a participant in his chosen exchange program. At last, it had come together for him: his essay, resume, and references all spoke of a young man who was qualified and prepared for this fellowship. We met again at a dinner I was invited to following his pre-departure orientation.

"You told me to keep trying, and I did," he said. He praised my teaching, let me know that my university missed me, and then added something that both pleased and startled me: "Most of all, you taught me how to be a good person."

I said that he deserved it because of his own hard work, and that I was proud of him. Several weeks later, he was on his way for a year of study in America.

※

I lost touch with Kairat after that, and I have no idea how his experience went or what he has done since then. For reasons that were numerous, complex, and intertwined, I decided to leave my position as a fellowship manager. I can't point to one reason more than any other; it was the sum of them together that convinced me it was time to move on.

It was a somewhat stressful period for foreign NGOs in Kazakhstan. New changes to numerous Kazakhstani laws on everything from mass demonstrations to media to NGOs were being proposed under the rubric of "national security." These included requiring that all foreign organizations print their annual financial reports in the newspaper and that anyone receiving a grant from a foreign organization report it to the government. There was already seemingly a law on everything. For example, one day someone was going to print our acceptance letters in color to show off our letterhead, but she had to be stopped because there was a law against printing in color when the letter included an electronic signature.

In one of the more bizarre stories concocted, the official government position was that the recent AIDS epidemic was the fault of foreigners, even though a report from the World Health Organization at the time implicated Kazakhstani injecting drug users and sex workers. As a result, I was required to be tested for AIDS every time I applied for a new visa. And with the red tape limiting work visas to six months, I ended up being AIDS tested three times within a one-year span.

None of this was enough for me to leave. I was, after all, living well in the country's cultural capital. One of the reasons was actually positive: my writing started to receive some encouraging recognition. I had been submitting my work from overseas and published in a few good journals and anthologies, even won a significant award. To fully embrace this would involve some risks. After talking it over with my wife, we decided that we would face those risks together, that she would support my decision to more deeply commit to my writing and return to teaching.

Sometimes we must step out of our comfort zones and explore new places. Sometimes we must step out of our comfort zones and return home.

⋇

When I arrived back in the States after nearly four years living overseas, I found that much had changed in that time. Everyone now owned cell phones and was soon chatting away on the new social media platforms. Twitter went live the very day I returned, while Facebook followed a few months later, yet I didn't notice healthier communication or a stronger feeling of community. It was a strange sensation. Something was different. I couldn't put my finger on it at first, but I could tell that the national air, our collective attitude, had shifted. We were embroiled in two large-scale wars, the economy was shaky, and politics had become more divisive than I had ever seen. Where a phrase I had never cared for, "us versus them," had once been used to describe Americans versus those in some other country, it was now being used to describe certain Americans against certain other Americans. This last portion especially caught me off guard. Obviously, the change had been developing slowly. To me, having been away for so long literally halfway around the world, it seemed to have happened overnight.

I probably hadn't been paying close enough attention before. Living overseas not only expands our vision by exposing us to a new culture, it helps us see our own culture better.

Once, when I was in Kazakhstan, an astute, intelligent, and professional young man responded to my comments about corruption in his country.

"Your country has just as much corruption," he said. "Only here it's out in the open while there it's hidden."

Though he had recently spent time in the United States and so knew it from firsthand experience, I disagreed with him—my own cultural conditioning led me automatically to reject his statement, even as I knew of my country's shortcomings. Now I wish I could meet that young man again and tell him that out of pride I had spoken too quickly. He was right. We're ostensibly a democracy, but too often our government is run by special interests. Lax campaign financing laws have made it easy for big money to flow into our legislative chambers. Tax breaks routinely favor the wealthiest and most powerful, while those most in need among us have seen programs to assist them slashed and eliminated. Gerrymandering and voter suppression are both employed to overrule the democratic will of the people.

On top of that, issues I had thought were well behind us, such as racism and sexism, have flared on our cultural skin like pustules full of bacteria, ready to burst. Xenophobia is a growing tumor, threatening to strangle our nation's heart. People in important government positions are pushing for building a physical wall around our borders. This goes against everything I believe in and deeply care about: openness and cooperation, mutual understanding forged through diplomacy and an exploration of shared interests, the free exchange of cultural ideas, fairness and equality—everything that prompted me to join the Peace Corps and seek out connections with others I knew nothing about and came to call my colleagues, allies, and friends. Would Kairat—or Julia, or Elena, or Anton, or any of my former students—feel welcome here in certain parts of the country today?

Yet simply how to begin addressing the issues we face, let alone formulate the kind of broad-based, community-focused solutions needed and then implement them, seems overwhelming. Just as my students felt helpless to change anything in their country, many people in my country, including me, now feel helpless to change what seems a gigantic, impersonal, well-protected, and immovable system.

It may be natural to believe certain things are out of our control, unavoidable sometimes if we want to get anything done or get anywhere in life. But people can and do change—and so can and do societies.

Thinking of my work overseas has helped, and Kairat's words still occasionally come back to me: "you taught me how to be a good person." I can only guess what he meant exactly, but I've thought about it a lot, and I feel it might be a recognition that trying is a virtue the same as being honest. And that trying for something you deeply care about, even when it seems unreachable, is a form of being honest with and honoring yourself.

I want to think he recognized that we can't always get what we want on the first try, and that the reason for this sometimes is that we aren't as ready as we think and others are simply better qualified; that we can build upon and build up our own qualifications, change who we are and become that better person we aspire to be; that all this takes not just a willingness on our parts but real effort over time; and that these concrete efforts define us, at least in part, as "good."

I don't know any of this for sure. I do know that in thinking about it, the tables have been turned, and Kairat's words are now doing the teaching, showing me something of myself. When I taught in Kazakhstan, I had always tried to aim high but content myself with the small victories, to take each day one at a time, each student one by one. Somehow, quietly, without my even knowing it, it had added up to something more.

We all have much work to do around the world and here at home: healing our badly wounded environment, cleaning up the way we do business, closing the chasm between the few very rich and the increasingly many poor, finding a way to live with other countries—or even our own neighbors—in peace. It can seem an overwhelming task. Change can come slowly, much more slowly than idealists with high expectations would like, and often it seems that in doing our own little parts, we're doing nothing at all. We must look past such seeming appearances, remain patient and true to our individual visions, and keep working anyway. We all have unique talents and experiences we can offer in service to each other, whether actively or behind the scenes. A sane, safe, just, and prosperous world for all is not going to magically appear on its own. We have to create it.

PLACE AS SELF

The places in our lives are rarely fixed, even relatively to us, like the polestar. Places are more often like comets, or rivers. They have elliptical orbits. They move, and their channels move over time as well. Sometimes they flood, and sometimes they dry up altogether. The change may happen quickly—an earthquake—or it may happen gradually, as with mountains, whose aging is best appreciated by studying series, erathem, and eonothem—the geologic strata of epochs, eras, and eons.

Ordinarily, however, we think that we can point to any particular place, as if locating it in space roots it in reality. There it is, we say. That mountain. Or that city, factory, graveyard. But time passes, and the next time we look, we see that a wildfire roared over the mountain one fine spring day when the wind was stretching its limbs uphill, and now the mountain is an unrecognizable old man. A six-lane superhighway runs through a neighborhood we once knew and loved. The house band at the local tavern packed up and left, even the double bass player, the tall, big-boned cat with the gray, stubbled beard who used to bring his bass fiddle in a bag with him on the bus, standing near the door with his arm around his instrument like a lover. The factory closed. The cemetery is choked with weeds.

Even the act of naming, often an effective way to pinpoint, define, and understand something (not to mention claim ownership of it), can be of limited value when writing about place. When we say "New York," do we mean the New York of, say, 1951, proud city of the Yankees, Dodgers, and Giants, or do we mean the New York of 2001, right after 9/11? As writers, we face a Zen riddle of a task: how to portray accurately what can't be named, can't be seen, can't even be found except in our memories, for inevitably, every place we write about has vanished irrevocably before we can pull out our notebooks and lick the tips of our pencils.

Still, we must do our best.

For four years, I lived in Kazakhstan, a region Genghis Khan ravaged pitilessly in the thirteenth century. While one of history's worst mass murderers has been dead for some eight hundred years, the seed of his possibly thousands of offspring spread wide. Even today, many ethnic Kazakhs can tell whether they are "white bone" or "black bone"—directly descended from Genghis Khan or not. Moreover, they can claim descent from a specific clan; important business transactions are often made or broken based on clan affiliation. Not every Kazakh cares about his or her heritage in this way. It may be—and in fact almost always is—something I never mention in my creative nonfiction, but I need to consider it nonetheless when writing about the relationships between people there.

So despite the limitations of language, knowing the details—the journalistic who, what, where, when, why, and how—is important. Even more important is conveying the spirit of a place. This is much trickier, and it's what makes creative nonfiction an art. There are no formulas to follow, though possessing a keen sense of intuition, love of adventure, and readiness to pack the mental bags and follow a hunch on a moment's notice all help. We've got to be able to travel lightly and take notes on the run.

At other times, because places don't stay in place, an almost preternatural patience is required. We wait and watch, hoping for the truth to pass by. But quantum physics recognizes the "observer effect," where what is being observed actually changes depending on who is doing the observing and how they are doing so. In the literature, this is well illustrated by comparing Ella Maillart's *Forbidden Journey* with Peter Fleming's *News from Tartary*, two classic but very different accounts of the same trip through Central Asia. We peer into our memories as scientists into electron microscopes, fully intending to remain impartial, faithful to truth, but in the end, we can only record what we ourselves experienced and saw.

The observer effect is closely linked with the "uncertainty principle." This states that when examining the physical properties of something, such as its position and velocity, we can only know one property more precisely at the expense of knowing the other less so. That's why light is sometimes seen as a particle and sometimes as a wave. Or why many people find rainy days depressing but such days make me feel happy. Seattle and London aren't for every writer.

This leads us to a variation of an old Zen riddle: if a place isn't experienced or even observed by a human, does it exist?

While in theory, places—entire universes of them—exist wholly independent of human exploration and observation (some might say contamination), in terms of creative nonfiction, a place exists *only* when it's been described in some form. Kazakhstan has existed by one name or another for millennia. Yet *my* Kazakhstan—the Kazakhstan I experienced as a foreigner, with my foreigner's values, prejudices, and occasionally clear-headed views, a vibrant, exotic, and challenging country tied inextricably to my thoughts and feelings of it—would never be known to anybody if I didn't describe it, which I've primarily done in my writing.

But already that world has become a museum piece, a scientific curiosity, a mammoth leg encased in ice. Examining a place in a particular time freezes portions of it. Our writing then becomes like an archival film. When done well, it imparts the illusion of life in seamless motion, but when scrutinized more closely, large gaps can be seen between the still frames. We can never reproduce all of life in our work, nor would we want to, only those moments that impart its essence. Good writers know this, and that's why what's left out is just as important as what's included. Much can be implied in the jumps between frames—between paragraphs, sections, chapters. Good writing is infused with an energy that carries readers over those jumps.

Of writing scenes, a teacher of mine once said, "Remember to save a place at the table for one who is missing." In Kazakhstan, ghosts of its Soviet past lurk everywhere. When writing about that country, I often pull up a chair for the Soviet Union and watch how my "characters"—those people I knew and still know there—react to it. Some are drawn almost helplessly toward the empty space, longing for what once physically occupied it; others act angry and others still bored or disinterested. No one explicitly says a thing. All are aware of the spirit in their midst.

Of course, we change just as places do. Buddhists believe that the self is nothing more than a constantly evolving aggregate of spatial and temporal elements, each also continually in flux. Thus, it's natural that our relationship to a particular place also changes each time we visit it. It changes again when we actually live there, and yet again when we leave. Distance in time changes it, as do our thoughts about it. Each time we write about it, it becomes a little more vivid in our minds, more clearly delineated and understandable—or it becomes indistinct due to all our thinking about it, more convoluted, an impenetrable puzzle. Regardless, it's different from what it was before, every time.

In this sense, place is very much like a character, and the best writers often treat it as such, as something with a personality of its own and, yes, even a will. (Think of Barry Lopez's work here.) When reading masters of creative nonfiction—Lopez, Gretel Ehrlich, John McPhee, and Wendell Berry are a few of my contemporary favorites—we can't help but to be drawn to the places they write of as if drawn to another human, a kindred soul. We see our own faces in the faces of the lands they so exquisitely portray.

Similarly, through our own work, we find ourselves tied to place in an inextricable way, for when writing about place, we seek not so much to define that place but to determine our place in it and in the larger world. The continually changing nature of place provides limitless possibilities for our explorations, not only of the places we write about but also of ourselves. We are born of particular places, live in them, love in them, and are otherwise marked by them even as we leave our marks upon them. As they change, we inevitably change with them, if not physically then at least in our hearts and minds. The places in our lives are part of the constantly evolving aggregate of who we are.

VIEW FROM A BRIDGE

I had only been living in Kazakhstan for a month when I made a trip from my home village of Kainazar to Esik, a larger town with a bustling bazaar. While crossing a bridge linking the bazaar's two halves, I suddenly stopped and looked up the narrow river valley to the peaks of the Tian Shan, so high above the town they were capped in snow even in July. I breathed in the myriad country smells of fresh mountain air, dust, roasting meat, the river rushing beneath me, the people pushing past me, and I felt an overpowering sense that I was exactly where I should have been. This sense came to me often during my time in the country, particularly those first two years as a Peace Corps English instructor. It was odd but exhilarating to feel nostalgic for a moment while it was happening, not after it had passed. In many ways, I never lived so fully in the moment as I did while in Kazakhstan.

It was only after I returned to America, however, that I was fully able to appreciate my experience overseas. I can now see it in a broader context, which has helped me better understand my adopted culture, my own culture, the importance of community, and the connections between them. I'm aided greatly by my Kazakhstani wife Valentina, and by my memories.

For example, once while standing in line at the post office, I met an immigrant woman who spoke Russian. As the clerk in front of us dealt with some business, we chatted about the same things two strangers anywhere might: our families, work, waiting in line.

"On tak medlenno rabotaet," she said—"He's working so slowly." I had to laugh, for when I lived in Kazakhstan, that's exactly how I felt about the postal workers there. It irked me when they took afternoon breaks together to drink tea, no matter the length of the lines at the windows. *Why don't they rotate breaks so that each worker goes one at a time?* I used to wonder with my typical American penchant for efficiency. I eventually came to understand that this would disrupt the communal aspect of drinking tea, something extremely important to Kazakhstanis. In general, food in Kazakhstan isn't simply for bodily sustenance; it's a means to sustain social connections. No holiday or other special occasion passes without a great gathering of family and friends, tables arranged so fully there isn't space for one more dish or glass. Kushai, kushai! comes the refrain in Russian—Eat, eat!—along with long, repeated toasts to everyone's health and prosperity running all through the evening and into the night.

And the food is fresh. I didn't appreciate just how fresh until I returned to America and had difficulty finding fruits and vegetables with any vitality to them. They look good here—large, colorful, unblemished—but curiously possess little flavor and are often unripe, the result of being picked early in order to be shipped long distances. Valentina cried after eating several purchases of deceptively beautiful red strawberries.

"They taste like raw potatoes," she said.

Very few of our communities produce their own food anymore. In Kazakhstan, fruits and vegetables are sold in the bazaar only in season, and they are often grown by the very babushki (grandmothers) who sell them. I loved haggling over the prices, listening to the pride each woman took in telling how her produce was the best. Meat is often butchered right in front of the customer. To the uninitiated, as I was at first, the smell in that section of the bazaar can be overwhelming, but I came to appreciate how the meat came straight from the farmer to the butcher (sometimes the same person) to me. I knew what I was eating. I hadn't thought as deeply about these issues before living in Kazakhstan. I've since become a strong advocate of organic, locally grown food.

I've also found myself longing to take afternoon breaks for a fresh pot of green tea, preferably with my wife. I'm usually not able to do so; American society isn't set up to accommodate this. Rather, it emphasizes multitasking to an unhealthy degree. When Americans go on break, even for lunch, we often check emails or run errands, gulping down food on the run, isolated from other humans. We could learn from the Kazakhstanis in this regard. I don't wish to oversimplify the situation. America offers a tremendous range of opportunities and choices, while Kazakhstan is still a developing country with many attendant problems: widespread poverty, crumbling infrastructure, corruption. Living there can be hard, as I personally experienced. But Kazakhstan has managed to keep some healthy traditions alive. People work better when they are refreshed and made to feel human, part of a human community. Afternoon tea almost magically restores such feelings.

When Valentina and I lived in Kentucky, we visited a quiet monastic community in a rural part of the state, Gethsemani Abbey, where the writer Thomas Merton lived and produced most of his voluminous and exquisitely beautiful work. Walking the trails of the abbey grounds that led along hayfields and into the woods, I sensed something hauntingly familiar.

"Do you smell that?" I asked. We both stopped and sniffed the air. A farmer was running a baling machine in a neighboring field, and the scent of fresh-cut hay mingled with that of the dusty path under our feet, horse dung, and blooming wildflowers. I felt as if I were again with my host family—Itam, Farida, and their children Malik, Adik, and Takmina—in the village where I had trained, or sitting behind the house where I learned Russian, in the shade by a cold mountain brook.

"This smells just like Kainazar."

"Yes, it does," Valentina agreed, gesturing around her. "We have this same grass and these same flowers in Kazakhstan."

Instead of the snow-peaked Tian Shan, we were surrounded by the green knobs of Kentucky, the colorful bazaar replaced by the Gethsemani Welcome Center and Gift Shop down the road. Two different periods of my life in two different cultures on opposite sides of the earth merged in that moment and became one. Just as I used to feel an odd but exhilarating nostalgia for moments as they were happening in Kazakhstan, so do I now often feel that curious but satisfying dislocation of time and place.

To say that I've bridged two cultures isn't the perfect metaphor. True, my experiences have helped me cross from my past to my present. But experiences don't stand alone. As with bridges, other people help build them. They become important parts of the landscape, both physical and spiritual. I can trace my path in the lines on my face and hands, in the lines of my memory. Four years of mountain wind helped carve them, along with steppe sun, laughter, and sometimes tears. More than fifteen years have now passed since I left Kazakhstan, yet in my emails and social media posts to friends and former colleagues there, I engineer spans that drop me off at their doorsteps and welcome them into my new home here in America. That bridge in Esik isn't the metaphor for my life in Kazakhstan as much as the people who continue to cross it back and forth every day, the surrounding bazaar, the entire town, the country itself. The cultural represents the personal, just as I, in my own small, individual way, once represented American culture as a Peace Corps volunteer.

I initially thought that in crossing from one culture to another and back I would arrive somewhere—full circle, if nothing else. I never did. I'm still somewhere in the middle, enjoying the view, something much different and far more enchanting than I could have seen or even imagined had I remained on the shore, drawn by the rushing waters but afraid to step out over them.

POSTOYANSTVO PAMYATI

(The Persistence of Memory)

The sound itself is ordinary all over the world, even in many urban areas in the States, and it can come in any season, but if everything else is just right—honey-colored light slanting through early-morning window or screen of trees, mugginess in air, day already beginning to swelter with heat, time stretching as it does for children and artists—then no matter where I might be, the rough, repeated crowing of a rooster instantly transports me to green foothills between the perennially snow-peaked Tian Shan and the vast arid steppe during my summer Peace Corps training in a small and remote village in Kazakhstan, when Itam was still alive, my entire host family and I gathered on the raised tapchan in their outdoor kitchen for rice porridge or eggs, shared tandoor-baked lepyoshka bread, and tea.

Bibliography

While I consulted scores of sources during my research for this book, I have listed only the most essential or broadly relevant here by media type for the sake of convenience.

Books

'Ali, 'Abdullah Yusuf. *The Meaning of the Holy Qur'an*. 10th ed. Beltsville, MD: Amana Publications, 1999.

Epstein, Mikhail. *After the Future: The Paradoxes of Postmodernism and Contemporary Russian Culture.* Amherst: The University of Massachusetts Press, 1995.

Haeri, Shaykh Fadhlalla. *The Elements of Sufism*. New York: Barnes & Noble Books, 1999. First published 1990 by Element Books.

Haneef, Suzanne. *What Everyone Should Know About Islam and Muslims.* 14th ed. Des Plaines, IL: Library of Islam, 1996.

Hanks, Reuel R. *Central Asia: A Global Studies Handbook*. Santa Barbara, CA: ABC-CLIO, 2005.

Holy Bible, New International Version. Revised ed. Grand Rapids, MI: Zondervan Publishing Co., 1984.

Khalid, Adeeb. *Islam after Communism: Religion and Politics in Central Asia.* Berkeley: University of California Press, 2007.

Kobori, Iwao and Michael H. Glantz, eds. *Central Eurasian Water Crisis: Caspian, Aral, and Dead Seas.* Tokyo: The United Nations University Press, 1998.

Loewen, James. *Lies My Teacher Told Me.* New York: Touchstone, 1996.

Louw, Maria Elisabeth. *Everyday Islam in Post-Soviet Central Asia.* London: Routledge, 2007.

Reznichenko, Grigory. *Aralskaya Katastrofa.* Moscow: Novosti, 1992.

Rippin, Andrew, ed. *The Islamic World.* London: Routledge, 2008.

Ruffin, M. Holt and Daniel C. Waugh, eds. *Civil Society in Central Asia.* Seattle: University of Washington Press, 1999.

Stoddart, William. *Outline of Sufism: The Essentials of Islamic Spirituality.* Bloomington, Ind.: World Wisdom, 2012.

Strasser, Andrea, Siegfried Haas, Gerhard Mangott, and Valeria Heuberger, eds. *Central Asia and Islam.* Hamburg: Deutsches Orient-Institut, 2002.

Sultanova, Razia. *From Shamanism to Sufism: Women, Islam and Culture in Central Asia.* London: I.B. Tauris, 2014.

Zarcone, Thierry and Angela Hobart, eds. *Shamanism and Islam: Sufism, Healing Rituals and Spirits in the Muslim World.* London: I.B. Tauris, 2013.

Book chapter

Kapuściński, Ryszard. "Central Asia—the Destruction of the Sea." In *Imperium.* New York: Vintage International, 1995: 254-264.

Articles, print

Klötzli, Stefan. "The Water and Soil Crisis in Central Asia: A Source for Future Conflicts?" Environment and Conflicts Project (ENCOP) Occasional Paper No. 11. Center for Security Studies. Zurich: Swiss Federal Institute of Technology, 1994.

Micklin, Philip P. "Desiccation of the Aral Sea: A Water Management Disaster in the Soviet Union." *Science* 241 (1988): 1170-1176.

Articles, Web

Gaybullaev, Behzod, Su-Chin Chen, and Dilmurod Gaybullaev. "Changes in Water Volume of the Aral Sea after 1960." *Applied Water Science* 2 (2012): 285-291. https://doi.org/10.1007/s13201-012-0048-z

Morris, Bridget. "The Death of the Aral Sea." *The Multinational Monitor* 11.9 (September 1990). https://multinationalmonitor.org/hyper/issues/1990/09/morris.html

Sun, Fangdi, and Ronghua Ma. "Hydrologic Changes of Aral Sea: A Reveal by the Combination of Radar Altimeter Data and Optical Images." *Annals of GIS* 25.3 (2019): 247-261. https://doi.org/10.1080/19475683.2019.1626909

Waugh, Daniel. "Samarkand and the Silk Road in the Time of the Timurids and Their Heirs." March 16, 2002. https://depts.washington.edu/silkroad/lectures/wulec5.html

Journals & Newspapers

Central Asia-Caucasus Analyst. https://cacianalyst.org/

Los Angeles Times. https://www.latimes.com

Silk Road. https://edspace.american.edu/silkroadjournal/

Time. https://time.com/

Times of Central Asia. https://www.timesca.com/

The Washington Times. https://www.washingtontimes.com/

Web sites

BBC News. https://www.bbc.com

Eurasianet. https://eurasianet.org/

Freedom House. https://freedomhouse.org/

International Dunhuang Project. http://idp.bl.uk/

International Religious Freedom Reports. https://www.state.gov/international-religious-freedom-reports/

Radio Free Europe/Radio Liberty. https://www.rferl.org

Silkroad Foundation. http://www.silkroadfoundation.org

Silk Road Seattle. https://depts.washington.edu/silkroad/

United Nations World Water Development Report Archives. https://www.unwater.org/publication_categories/world-water-development-report/

World Water Forum. https://www.worldwatercouncil.org/en/world-event

World Wildlife Fund. https://www.worldwildlife.org/

About the Author

Image: Sabina Poole for the Oregon Arts Commission

Jeff Fearnside is the author of the short-story collection *Making Love While Levitating Three Feet in the Air* and the chapbook *A Husband and Wife Are One Satan*, winner of the Orison Chapbook Prize.

Other awards for his writing include a Grand Prize in the Santa Fe Writers Projects Literary Awards Program, the Mary Mackey Short Story Prize, and an Individual Artist Fellowship from the Oregon Arts Commission. His work has appeared in numerous literary journals and anthologies, such as *The Paris Review*, *Los Angeles Review*, *Story*, *The Pinch*, *The Sun*, and *Everywhere Stories: Short Fiction from a Small Planet*.

Fearnside lived in Central Asia for four years and has travelled widely along the Great Silk Road. He has taught writing and literature at the Academy of Languages in Kazakhstan and various institutions in the U.S.